Threads
of History

TEACHER'S COMPANION RESOURCE

A Thematic Approach
to Our Nation's Story
for AP* U.S. History

by Michael Henry, Ph.D.

SHERPALEARNING
GUIDING YOU TO EVEN GREATER HEIGHTS

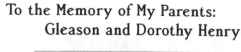

To the Memory of My Parents:
Gleason and Dorothy Henry

Publisher: David Nazarian

Editor: Richard Carson

Cartographer: Sal Esposito

The publisher would like to thank Dan Frederiks, U.S. History teacher extraordinaire.

Cover Image: Map Quilt (detail); Artist unidentified; Possibly Virginia, 1886; Silk and cotton with silk embroidery; 78 3/4 x 82 1/4"; Collection American Folk Art Musuem, New York; Gift of Dr. and Mrs. C. David McLaughlin; 1987.1.1; Photo by Schecter Lee, New York

Image Credits: p. 165, The introduction of African slavery into the American colonies at Jamestown, Virginia, August, 1619, wood engraving, late 19th century, The Granger Collection, New York City; p. 171, cartoon of the Ninth National Women's Rights Convention, May 12, 1859, Harper's Weekly, June 11, 1859; p. 177, "A Giant Straddle," by William Allen Rogers, Harper's Weekly, March 28, 1896;

* AP is a registered trademark of the College Board, which was not involved in the production of, and does not endorse, this product.

Common Core State Standards © Copyright 2010. National Governors Association Center for Best Practices and Council of Chief State School Officers. All rights reserved.

ISBN 978-0-9905471-1-2

Copyright © 2015

Sherpa Learning, LLC.

West Milford, New Jersey

www.sherpalearning.com

SHERPALEARNING
GUIDING YOU TO EVEN GREATER HEIGHTS

Printed in the United States of America.

10 9 8 7 6 5 4 3

Threads of History

2nd Edition

The Long Essay Questions and Suggested Responses

The Document-Based Questions and Suggested Responses

Appendices

Preface to the Teacher's Companion Resource

To my Friends and Colleagues,

Thanks for purchasing the updated and revised 2nd Edition of *Threads of History*! This Teacher's Companion Resource is designed to help you evaluate and deepen your students' understanding of the thirty-five charts that are the heart of the Student Edition. This will also serve as a guide to the rest of the materials and resources offered in the Student Edition and on the Teacher's Companion Website. I hope that these materials will prove to be effective instructional tools for you throughout the school year as you prepare your students for the challenge of the exam and for the demands of college.

Preparing the for the New Exam

The AP* United States History exam will change significantly for 2015 and beyond. The emphasis of the multiple-choice section will shift from recall and application to the use of source materials in order to test historical thinking skills. However, students will be asked to use both the sources and historical knowledge to answer the multiple-choice questions. In addition, the short-answer questions will require students to draw from a sound factual base in order to think thematically and more abstractly.

While thinking skills will be important on the test, students must still have relevant historical knowledge to fuel their thinking. Students can only reason historically if they have facts and ideas with which to reason. Without specific information about America's past, students will fail to identify the relationships asked for by the multiple-choice questions and be reduced to vague generalities and misrepresentations on the short answer and long essay questions. The thematic charts in the lessons of the Student Edition will help your students develop some of the factual base necessary to succeed on the examination.

How to Use This Book

The Student Edition of *Threads of History* is designed to help your students develop essential skills so that you can focus more on covering the content. The resources in this companion text, however, are designed to make it as easy as possible for you to integrate *Threads* into your existing curriculum plan. What follows is a guide to the resources found within this text. After that, you will find a guide to the materials on the Teacher's Companion Website.

The Lesson Plans

The first part of this Companion Resource contains a series of ten lesson plans based on topics developed in ten of the charts found in the Student Edition. These lesson plans are designed to be completed in a fifty-minute class period, and should prove useful to you throughout the year as the topics are covered in your course.

Title	Lesson Number	Student Edition Primary Source	Lesson Plan Primary Source
Famous Rebellions	2	Letter from Washington to Madison	Bacon's Manifesto
Presidents of the United States, 1789–2001	4	Jefferson speech, 1801	Bryce's "Why Great Men are Not Chosen President"
Coming of the American Revolution	6	Inglis's "The True Interest of America Impartially Stated"	*Same, but extended*
Compromises and the Union	13	John C. Calhoun speech, 1850	*Same, but extended*
Expanding Democracy—The Abolitionist Movement	20	Garrison's "Declaration of Sentiments of the America Anti-Slavery Convention"	Child's "Colonization Society and Anti-Slavery Society"
Judicial Betrayal—The Road to *Plessy v. Ferguson*	24	Civil Rights Cases, 1883	Harlan's dissenting opinion for *Plessy v. Ferguson*
Black Leaders, 1880–1968	27	Malcolm X, press conference, 1964	*Same, but extended*
Isolationism vs. Internationalism	30	Nye's "Is Neutrality Possible for America?"	*Same, but extended*
Containment, 1945–1975	33	*Minneapolis Star* cartoon, "Step on it, Doc!" 1947	National Security Council Paper 68
Failure of Containment—The Vietnam War	34	Veterans for Peace rally photo, San Francisco, 1969	Letter from Eisenhower to Ngo Dinh Diem

Each lesson plan uses information from a chart to provide an introduction to the activity. Building on this introductory material, a primary source document is presented on one aspect of the topic developed in the chart. A series of questions about the document is provided to promote class discussion and encourage student inquiry into the issues raised by the chart.

The primary source documents in the lesson plans are available on the website in PDF format so that you can easily project them in class or duplicate them for your students. Four of the lesson plans use the same documents as in the Source Activities of the corresponding lessons in the Student Edition. These lesson plans will extend/deepen student interaction with those documents.

Answers and Explanations for the Source Activities

The Source Activities in each lesson will help students develop and improve historical "habits of the mind"—the dispositions that include generating a plan of action to solve problems, accessing reliability of information, identifying point-of-view, and recognizing the relationship between facts and larger historical contexts. These exercises, while not attempting to precisely replicate questions that appear on the test, do anticipate many of the reasoning skills that are needed for students to be successful in the course, on the exam, and beyond!

The Essay Questions and Suggested Responses

The next two sections of this guide offer detailed answers to the 17 long essay questions and the 3 document-based questions found on the Teacher Companion Website. The long essay questions are designed to assess students' understanding of topics and themes presented in one or more of the charts. The document-based questions have the rare quality of having never been published on a past exam.

We intentionally withheld the LEQ and DBQ prompts from inclusion in the Student Edition because we felt (and our reviewers agreed) that teachers would want to use them in quizzes and tests. Therefore, it would be best if the students were not able to view them in advance. The questions are available on the Teacher Companion Website in PDF format, so that you can easily print and distribute them to your students. They are also available in Microsoft Word format, should you want to copy/paste them into your own quizzes and tests.

The suggested response outlines identify themes, interpretations, and facts that students might include in a well-developed response. The outlines are very detailed, so it is extremely unlikely that students would include all of the themes and information listed. These outlines are offered as guidelines to help assist you as you construct your own classroom grading standards and hopefully make it easier for you to grade your students' essays.

The essay questions can be used in several ways in your APUSH class. You may wish to assign the questions during the year as either in-class or out-of-class writing activities when the topics are presented in your curriculum. In this format, the questions could serve as measures of current student learning. They would provide an index of how much students have understood about the historical period they have just studied. You might also use one or more essay questions on a midterm or final examination to determine how much knowledge and understanding students have retained throughout the semester or year. Finally, several of the questions, in conjunction with multiple-choice items from the online test bank, could be used as part of a practice exam that you design.

The Rubrics

The College Board rubrics for the LEQs and DBQs are somewhat complex and may require a period of adjustment for some teachers. In order to facilitate this, I have included simplified guides to aid in the successful utilization of the College Board rubrics in your assessment of student responses. These simplifications use a three-step process that is intended to help with the transition to the new rubrics for both essay formats. The first step of the process is a quick summary of each component of the rubric. The second provides an annotative version of the rubric to be used in the early part of the year. Finally, step 3 provides a basic, at-a-glance version of the rubric that can be used as a quick grading reference once the grading process is more comfortable.

The Distribution Charts

Four distribution charts have been provided to help you effectively utilize the wealth of practice items contained in *Threads of History* and the online test bank.

The first chart identifies practice items by the major chronological periods of the APUSH course. This chart is designed to help you build quizzes and practice activities that perfectly sync with your curriculum plan.

The second and third charts identify practice items by the corresponding Learning Objectives and Historical Thinking Skills provided by the College Board in the redesigned APUSH course framework. These charts are designed to make it easy for you to identify and target areas where your students struggle to achieve the standards outlined by the College Board.

You'll notice that the questions that accompany the charts in each lesson are not correlated to the College Board's standards. These questions are designed to test specific knowledge and understandings directly related to the charts and, as such, do not cleanly align to the intents of the Learning Objectives and Historical Thinking Skills. They do, however, provide students with some of the information they will need to answer the questions posed about the primary sources, so they play a vital role in classroom instruction and preparation for the new types of multiple-choice questions they will encounter on the redesigned exam.

Finally, the fourth chart has been included to offer an overview of how this new edition of *Threads of History* aligns to the Common Core State Standards for History/Social Studies for grades 11-12. *Threads* was not designed with the CCSS in mind, yet it does an excellent job of addressing all 10 of these standards, some in greater depths than others.

Closing Thoughts

Again, I hope that these materials are a great help to you as you adjust to the new course and exam. If you have any questions about the materials, please raise them in the community forum on the Teacher Companion Website. If *Threads* has been a help to you and your students, please let us know! If you'd like to reach me personally, you can email me at mikehenryhistory@gmail.com. I'd love to hear from you.

Sincerely,

Michael Henry

Guide to the Website Resources

In addition to the abundance of content found in the Student Edition and this Teacher's Companion Resource, a substantial collection of valuable resources have been made available to you through the companion website, **http://threads.sherpalearning.com**. These items have been placed on the website because they are most useful in digital form; it will be easier for you to display with a projector, print and copy handouts, and copy/paste items for your custom tests and quizzes. This also makes it easier for you to share and distribute these items. **PLEASE DON'T**—not only because it's against the law, but because we cannot continue to provide quality resources like this without paying customers.

To access these resources on the companion website, please go to **http://threads. sherpalearning.com** and register your copy of *Threads of History* – Teacher's Companion Resource. Each copy of the TCR includes a label on the inside front cover with your unique identification code. If you misplace your code, or if your book happened to come without this label, please contact us at hello@sherpalearning.com and we'll get you straightened out.

The Threads Community

The companion website offers a forum for teachers to share their thoughts, questions, and ideas about the 2nd Edition of *Threads of History*. If you post to the forum, the website will email you an alert when there is a response to your post. It's a great way to share your strategies and success stories with your peers and hear about what techniques they are using in their classrooms.

Core Chart Worksheets

To get your students more comfortable with the data charts in the lessons, you might want to use the Core Chart Workseets. These are the same as the data charts found in some of the lessons, however, most of the cells have been left blank. Have your students fill in the blank cells in the charts, either in groups or individually. This activity will require students to research various topics and themes presented in a chart, discuss these ideas, expand their meaning, and expand their understandings beyond the recall level.

Core Chart Worksheets have been provided for the following lessons:

Lesson 1	Historical Periods
Lesson 2	Famous Rebellions
Lesson 3	Religious Development, 1619–1740
Lesson 7	The National Banks
Lesson 12	Freedom of the Seas and Wars with Europe
Lesson 20	Expanding Democracy—The Abolitionist Movement
Lesson 24	Judicial Betrayal—The Road to *Plessy v. Ferguson*

The charts increase in rigor (more cells left blank) as the lessons progress.

HIPPO: Getting Ready for the DBQ

H.I.P.P.O. is a tool you can use at the beginning of the school year to help your students build document analysis and writing skills required to successfully answer the Document-Based Question. It focuses on the four components identified as necessary for the new DBQ. It also reminds students that they must do more than simply decode a document; they must apply it to a thesis or argument.

Worksheets for Source Activities

Appendix C in the Student Edition introduces students to the three primary source worksheets that should be used in conjunction with the Source Activities in each lesson. The three worksheets are available for printing and duplication on the website. These worksheets provide critical support as your students begin to develop document analysis skills.

The Online Test Bank

The test bank of multiple-choice questions available on the companion website will help you determine if your students have mastered the information. If they have not, identify the gaps in their understanding and hone in on exactly where each individual student needs to improve. Answering these questions will help your students know if they clearly understand a topic and build confidence in their ability to think critically, comprehensively, and comparatively.

Moving Forward

If you have success using any of these resources, please share your experiences in the Teacher Forum. If you know of additional resources that the rest of the *Threads* community might find useful, please share them. Sherpa Learning is eager to expand upon our offerings on the companion website, but only with your guidance. Let us know what you'd like to see more of, and we'll do our best to deliver. That's one of the many ways Sherpa Learning is trying to be different. So please, don't hold back!

If you'd like to learn more about Sherpa Learning and what we're all about, please go to our website: **www.sherpalearning.com**.

Lesson Plans

Lesson Plan

Famous Rebellions

R eview the introductory material and the chart "Three Major Rebellions in Early U.S. History" on pages 6 and 7 in the Student Edition (SE) of *Threads of History*. Have your students discuss what these rebellions (other than Nat Turner's) suggest about the American character. Can your students identify any common traits that contributed to the three uprisings?

OBJECTIVES

After the class discussion on rebellions and after reading "Nathaniel Bacon's Manifesto," which follows, students will be able to:

1. analyze the causes of Bacon's Rebellion;

2. compare the views of Bacon and governor Berkeley on the causes of the rebellion;

3. evaluate to what extent Bacon's Rebellion was a defense of colonial rights against insensitive British policies;

4. explain how the rebellion was viewed as a clash between the haves and the have-nots in Virginia.

DISCUSSION QUESTIONS

Hand out the article on page 3 and ask the following:

1. How does Bacon view himself and his supporters?

2. What oppressive acts does Bacon charge Governor Berkeley with? How do you think the governor would answer these charges?

3. Whom does Bacon call "juggling parasites"?

4. From your knowledge of the rebellion, which of its elements are not mentioned in Bacon's Manifesto?

5. How does Bacon attempt to make the rebellion a political and economic protest?

6. From this document and your knowledge of the rebellion, was Bacon the first American revolutionary or simply a blood-thirsty Indian hater?

Nathaniel Bacon's Manifesto

If virtue be a sin, if piety be guilt, all the principles of morality, goodness, and justice be perverted, we must confess that those who are now called rebels may be in danger of those high imputations. Those loud and several bulls [Governor Berkeley's declarations] would afright [sic] innocents and render the defense of our brethren, and the inquiry into our own sad and heavy oppressions, treason.

But if there be, as sure there is, a God to appeal to; if religion and justice be a sanctuary here; if to plead the cause of the oppressed; if sincerely to aim at this Majesty's honor and the public good without any reservation or by interest … [then] let God Almighty judge and let [the] guilty die.

But since we cannot in our hearts find one single spot of rebellion or treason, or that we have in any manner aimed at the subverting [of] the settled government, or attempting of the person of any either magistrate or private man, notwithstanding the several reproaches and threats of some who for sinister ends were disaffected to us and censured our innocent and honest designs; and since all people in all places where we have yet been can attest our civil, quiet and peaceable behavior, let truth be bold and all the world know the real foundation of pretended guilt …

But let us trace these men in authority and favor, to whose hands the dispensation of the country's wealth has been committed. Let us observe the sudden rise of their estates, composed [compared] with the quality in which they first entered this country, or the reputation they have held here amongst wise and discerning men. And let us see whether their extractions and educations have not been vile, and by what pretense of learning and virtue they could soon [enter] into employments of so great trust and consequences. Let us consider their sudden advancement and let us also consider whether any public work for our safety and defense … is here extant in any [way] adequate to our vast charge.

Now let us compare these things together and see what sponges have sucked up the public treasure, and whether it has not been privately contrived away by unworthy favorites and juggling parasites, whose tottering fortunes have been repaired and supported at the public charge.

Now if it be so, judge what greater guilt can be than to offer to pry into these and to unriddle [sic] the mysterious wiles of a powerful cabal. Let all people judge what can be of more dangerous import than to suspect the so long safe proceedings of some of our grandees, and whether people may with safety open their eyes in so nice a concern.

Lesson Plan 4

Presidents of the United States, 1789–2001

Review the introductory materials and the chart " The Four Great Presidents" on pages 14 and 15 in the Student Edition (SE) of *Threads*. Have your students discuss the four presidents identified as great. From the list of four, ask your students to select one president who stands out as the greatest of the great. Ask them to defend their answer.

OBJECTIVES

After the class discussion on presidential greatness and reading James Bryce's "Why Great Men Are Not Chosen Presidents," which follows, students will be able to:

1. defend their choice of America's greatest president;

2. identify the characteristics of a great president;

3. list several limitations and/or hurdles that block great men from achieving the presidency;

4. apply these limitations specifically to the political circumstances that defined presidential politics from 1868–1900.

DISCUSSION QUESTIONS

Hand out the article on page 5 and ask the following:

1. Is James Bryce an unbiased observer of American politics? (Focus on the statement, "Besides, most American voters do not object to ordinary candidates" in the article).

2. What factors did Bryce identify that restricted great men from achieving the presidency?

3. Examine the presidential greatness chart ("The Four Greatest Presidents") on page 15 of the Student Edition. How did these men overcome the hurdles Bryce mentioned to become great presidents?

4. Can you think of examples in the years 1868–1900 of men who "would make a good president, but a very bad candidate"?

5. Is it true that "a president need not be brilliant"?

6. What qualities does Bryce think a great president needs? Do you agree?

Why Great Men Are Not Chosen President

Europeans often ask, and Americans do not always explain, how it happens that this great office—to which any man can rise by his own merits—is not more frequently filled by great men … it might be expected that the presidency would always be won by a man of brilliant gifts. But since the heroes of the Revolution died out with Jefferson and Adams and Madison some sixty years ago, no person except General Grant has reached the office whose name would have been remembered if he had not been President. No President except Abraham Lincoln has shown rare or striking qualities in the office… .

Several reasons may be suggested for this fact, which Americans are themselves the first to admit.

One is that the number of people with great abilities drawn into politics is smaller in America than in most European countries. In France and Italy, half-revolutionary conditions have made public life exciting and easy to enter … In England, many persons of wealth and leisure seek to enter politics, while vital problems touch the interests of all classes and make people eager observers of the political scene. In America, many able men rush into a field which is comparatively small in Europe, the business of developing the material resources of the country.

Another reason is that the methods and habits of Congress and indeed of political life generally, seem to give fewer opportunities for personal distinction. There are fewer ways in which a man may win the admiration of his countrymen by outstanding thought, speech or ability in administration.

A third reason is that important men make more enemies than less well-known men do. They are therefore less admirable candidates … No man can be in public life for long and take part in great affairs without causing criticism …

… Besides, most American voters do not object to ordinary candidates. They have a lower idea of the qualities necessary for a statesman than those who direct public opinion in Europe … They do not value, because they see no need for, originality or profundity, a cultured background or great knowledge …

It must also be remembered that the merits of a President are one thing and those of a candidate another thing. An important American is reported to have said to friends … "Gentlemen, let there be no mistake. I would make a good President but a very bad candidate" … After all—and this is a point much less obvious to Europeans than to Americans—a President need not be brilliant … They forget that the President does not sit in Congress. His main duties are to promptly and effectively carry out the laws and maintain public order … Firmness, common sense, and, most of all, honesty are the qualities which the country needs in its chief executive.

Coming of the American Revolution

Review the introductory material and the chart "Acts, Actions, and Reactions Leading Up to the American Revolution" on pages 24 and 25 in the Student Edition (SE) of *Threads*. Have your students discuss whether the American Revolution was inevitable, given the English mercantile system and the colonial attitudes in 1776.

OBJECTIVES

After the class discussion on the inevitability of the Revolution and reading Charles Inglis's "The True Interest of America Impartially Stated, 1776," which follows, students will be able to:

1. outline the Loyalists' reasons for supporting British control of the colonies;

2. evaluate the economic basis for the Loyalists' position;

3. analyze why the Loyalists' point of view did not have more support in the colonies.

DISCUSSION QUESTIONS

Hand out the article on page 7 and ask the following:

1. How does Inglis attempt to appeal to national pride in making the case for staying with England?

2. What advantages does he see in the colonies' remaining under the British Empire?

3. How do you think the colonial rebels countered these arguments?

4. Why do you think Inglis believed "a republican form of government would neither suit the spirit of the people, nor the size of America"?

5. According to Inglis, what part of colonial life would be most affected by independence from England?

6. Why do you think the Loyalists' position had limited appeal in the colonies?

The True Interest of America Impartially Stated

By a settling of differences with Britain an end would be put to the present terrible war, by which so many lives have been lost, and so many more must be lost, if it continues. This alone is an advantage devoutly to be wished for. [Thomas] Paine says—"The blood of the slain, the weeping voice of nature cries. 'Tis time to part." I think they cry just the reverse. The blood of the slain, the weeping voice of nature cries—it is time to be reconciled.

By a connection with Great Britain, our trade would still have the protection of the greatest naval power in the world. The protection of our trade, while connected with Britain, will not cost us a fiftieth part of what it must cost, were we ourselves to raise a naval force sufficient for this purpose. The manufactures of Great Britain confessedly surpass any in the world... .

The advantages are not imaginary but real. They are such as we have already experienced; and such as we may derive from a connection with Great Britain for ages to come.

Suppose we were to revolt from Great Britain, declare ourselves Independent, and set up a Republic of our own—what would be the consequence?—I stand aghast at the prospect—my blood runs chill when I think of the calamities, the complicated evils that must follow... .

What a horrid situation would thousands be reduced to who have taken the oath of allegiance to the King. They must renounce that allegiance, or abandon all their property in America! By a Declaration of Independency, every avenue to a compromise with Great Britain would be closed. The sword only could decide the quarrel. And the sword would not be sheathed till one had conquered the other.

Devastation and ruin must mark the progress of this war along the sea coast of America. Hitherto, Britain has not exerted her power. Her number of troops and ships of war here at present, is very little more than she judged necessary in time of peace. The troops amount to no more than 12,000 men. The ships to no more than 40, including frigates. Both Great Britain and the colonies hoped for and expected compromise. Neither of them has lost sight of that desirable object.

But supposing once more that we were able to cut off every regiment that Britain can spare or hire, and to destroy every ship she can send. Suppose we could beat off any other European power that would presume to invade this continent. Yet, a republican form of government would neither suit the spirit of the people, nor the size of America.

13 Compromises and the Union

Review the introductory material and the chart "Four Major Compromises in U.S. History" on pages 54 and 55 in the Student Edition of *Threads*. Have your students discuss whether compromise is a positive or negative process in a republic. Focus on whether postponing the issue of slavery and its future was beneficial to the nation's well-being.

OBJECTIVES

After the class discussion on compromises and reading John C. Calhoun's March 4, 1850 speech, which follows, students will be able to:

1. outline the southern position on slavery and its spread in the 1850s;

2. describe the South's view of the Union in 1850;

3. evaluate the role of the abolitionists in bringing on the sectional crisis in antebellum America;

4. assess whether Calhoun's position in 1850 could forge the basis for a compromise over slavery.

DISCUSSION QUESTIONS

Hand out the article on page 9 and ask the following:

1. Whom does John Calhoun blame for most of the sectional troubles from 1830–1850? Do you agree with this view?

2. How does Calhoun explain the relative political strengths of the two sections? Do you agree with this view?

3. What is Calhoun's solution for solving the crisis in 1850?

4. From what you already know about Calhoun, is this consistent with his earlier views?

5. Given Calhoun's position, is compromise likely in 1850?

6. What events and developments from 1830–1850 brought John Calhoun to his point of view?

John C. Calhoun's Speech, March 4, 1850

A single section, governed by the will of the numerical majority, now controls the government [in] its entire powers. The North has absolute control over the government. It is clear, therefore, that on all questions between it and the South, where there are different interests, the interests of the South will be sacrificed to the North, no matter how oppressive the effects may be. The South possesses no political means by which it can resist.

Northern hostility towards the social organization of the South lay dormant a long time. The first organized movement against it began in 1835. Then, for the first time, antislavery societies were organized, presses established, lecturers sent forth to excite the people of the North, and incendiary publications were scattered over the whole South, through the mail... .

With the increase of their influence, the abolitionists extended the sphere of their action. In a short time, they had sufficient influence to get the legislatures of most of the northern states to pass acts which in effect repealed the provision of the Constitution that provides for the return of fugitive slaves. This was followed by petitions and resolutions of legislatures of the northern states and popular meetings, to exclude the southern states from all territories acquired or to be acquired, and to prevent the admission of any state into the Union which, by its constitution, does not prohibit slavery.

How can the Union be saved? There is but one way by which it can with any certainty; and that is, by a full and final settlement, on the principle of justice, of all the questions at issue between the two sections. The South asks for justice, simple justice, and less she ought not to take. She has no compromise to offer but the Constitution, and no concession or surrender to make. She has already surrendered so much that she has little left to surrender ...

But can this be done? Yes, easily; not by the weaker party, for it can of itself do nothing—not even protect itself—but by the stronger. The North has only to do justice by conceding to the South an equal right in the acquired territory to do her duty by causing the constitutional provisions related to fugitive slaves to be faithfully fulfilled, to cease the agitation of the slave question, and to provide for an amendment to the Constitution. Such an amendment should restore to the South the power she possessed to protect herself, before the balance between the section [sic] was destroyed by this government.

But will the North agree to this? It is for her to answer this question. But, I will say, she cannot refuse, if she has half the love of the Union which she professes to have, or without justly exposing herself to the charge that her love of power is far greater than her love of the Union. At all events, the responsibility of saving the Union rests on the North, and not the South.

Lesson Plan 20

Expanding Democracy— The Abolitionist Movement

Review the introductory materials and the chart "Strands of the Abolitionist Crusade" on pages 84 and 85 of the Student Edition of *Threads*. Have your students discuss why the colonization movement had support in the South but was an anathema to the northern abolitionists.

OBJECTIVES

After the class discussion on the colonization movement and reading Lydia Maria Child's "Colonization Society and Anti-Slavery Society," which follows, students will be able to:

1. explain the goals and methods of the abolitionists in the mid 1830s;

2. compare the ideas of the American Colonization Society to the anti-slavery ideas of William Lloyd Garrison and his supporters;

3. summarize the assumptions and beliefs of the abolitionists about race and the origins of slavery in America;

4. evaluate the overall impact of the abolitionists on America from 1830–1850.

DISCUSSION QUESTIONS

Hand out the article on page 11 and ask the following:

1. What was the objective of the abolitionists according to Child?

2. How did the abolitionists propose to reach this objective?

3. Why did the abolitionists oppose the colonization movement?

4. According to Child, what was the origin of racial prejudice in America? Do you agree with this interpretation?

5. What attitudes or assumptions about African Americans did the abolitionists profess to have?

6. Were the abolitionists a positive or negative force in America during the antebellum period?

Colonization Society and Anti-Slavery Society

The Colonization Society has fallen into the habit of glossing over the enormities of the slave system ... they have pledged themselves not to speak, write, or do anything to offend the Southerners, and as there is no possible way of making the truth pleasant to those who do not love it, the Society must perforce keep the truth out of sight... .

But so long as the South insists that slavery is unavoidable, and say they will not tolerate any schemes tending to its abolition—and so long as the North take [sic] the necessity of slavery for an unalterable truth, and put [sic] down any discussions, however mild and candid, which tend to show that it may be done away with safely—so long as we thus strengthen each other's hand in evil, what remote hope is there of emancipation? ... To enlighten public opinion is the best way that has been discovered for the removal of national evils, and slavery is certainly a national evil... .

My ... greatest objection to the Colonization Society is, that its members write and speak, both in public and private, as if the prejudice against skins darker colored than their own, was a fixed and unalterable law of our nature, which cannot possibly be changed ... we are constantly told ... that people of color ... never can have all the rights and privileges of citizens ... because the prejudice is so great...

This is shaking hands with iniquity, and covering sin with a silver veil. Our prejudice against the blacks is founded in sheer pride ... We made slavery, and slavery makes the prejudice. No Christian, who questions his own conscience, can justify himself in indulging the feeling. The removal of this prejudice is not a matter of opinion—it is a matter of duty... .

[We] lay it down as a maxim that immediate emancipation is the only just course, and the only safe policy ... no other course can be pursued which does not ... involve a constant violation of the laws of God... .

The Colonization Society are [sic] always reminding us that the master has rights as well as the slave; The Anti-Slavery Society urge [sic] us to remember that the slave has rights as well as the master. I leave it for somber sense to determine which of these claims is in the greatest danger of being forgotten.

Judicial Betrayal—
The Road to *Plessy v. Ferguson*

eview the introductory materials and the chart "Major Civil Rights Cases" on the judicial rulings that led to the *Plessy v. Ferguson* case in 1896 on pages 100 and 101 in the Student Edition of *Threads*. Have your students discuss the basic assumptions these court cases made about American society and the role of the federal government in race relations from 1873–1896.

OBJECTIVES

After the class discussion on the role of the courts in race relations after the Civil War and reading John Marshall Harlan's dissent which follows, students will be able to:

1. state the basic judicial principles on which the Jim Crow system was based;

2. explain how separate but equal became the law of the land in the first half of the twentieth century;

3. compare John Marshall Harlan's thinking on civil rights to the majority views on the Supreme Court;

4. evaluate the impact of *Plessy v. Ferguson* in creating the Jim Crow system in the United States;

5. assess John Marshall Harlan's role in American judicial history.

DISCUSSION QUESTIONS

Hand out the article on page 13 and ask the following:

1. What was Harlan's view of the Constitution and race relations?

2. Why does Harlan think the Constitution should be "color-blind"?

3. To what earlier court case does Harlan compare *Plessy*? Why do you think he makes this comparison?

4. What result does he think the *Plessy* decision will have on race relations in the United States?

5. Does the fact that Harlan was once a slaveholder change your opinion of his dissent? Why or why not?

Justice John Marshall Harlan's
Dissenting Opinion in *Plessy v. Ferguson*

In respect of civil rights, common to all citizens, the Constitution of the United States does not, I think, permit any public authority to know the race of those entitled to be protected in the enjoyment of such rights. ... But I deny that any legislative body or judicial tribunal may have regard to the race of citizens when the civil rights of those citizens are not involved. Indeed, such legislation, as that here in question, is inconsistent not only with the equality of rights which pertains to citizenship, National and State, but with the personal liberty enjoyed by everyone within the United States.

The white race deems itself to be the dominant race in this country. And so it is, in prestige, in achievements, in education, in wealth and in power. So I doubt not, it will continue to be for all time, if it remains true to its great heritage and holds fast to the principles of constitutional liberty. But in view of the Constitution, in the eye of the law, there is in this country no superior, dominant ruling class of citizens. There is no caste here. Our Constitution is color-blind, and neither knows nor tolerates classes among citizens. In respect of civil rights, all citizens are equal before the law... .

In my opinion, the judgment this day rendered will, in time, prove to be quite as pernicious as the decision made by this tribunal in the Dred Scott case ... The present decision, it may well be apprehended, will not only stimulate aggressions, more or less brutal and irritating, upon the admitted rights of colored citizens, but will encourage the belief that it is possible by means of state enactments, to defeat the beneficent purposes which the people of the United States had in view when they adopted the recent amendments to the Constitution, by one of which the blacks of this country were made citizens of the United States and of the States in which they respectively reside, and whose privileges and immunities, as citizens the States are forbidden to abridge. ... The destinies of the two races, in this country, are indissolubly linked together, and the interests of both require that the common government of all shall not permit the seeds of race hate to be planted under the sanction of law... .

I am of opinion that the statute of Louisiana is inconsistent with the personal liberty of citizens, white and black, in that State, and hostile to both the spirit and letter of the Constitution... .

Black Leaders, 1880–1968

Review the introductory materials and the chart "Influential Black Leaders" on pages 112 and 113 in the Student Edition of *Threads*. Have your students compare the debate between Booker T. Washington and W.E.B. Du Bois in the early twentieth century with the clashes between Martin Luther King Jr. and Malcolm X in the 1960s. Ask them to identify the man in each of these eras who was the most effective leader of black Americans at the time. Have students defend their answers.

OBJECTIVES

After the class discussion on black leadership and reading Malcolm X's news conference which follows, students should be able to:

1. compare and contrast the issue faced by African-Americans at midcentury with those they faced in the early 1900s;

2. summarize the philosophy of Malcolm X before his trip to Mecca;

3. evaluate Malcolm X as a civil rights leader;

4. explain the major differences between Martin Luther King Jr. and Malcolm X in 1964;

5. analyze how Malcolm X could appeal to groups of African Americans that other leaders failed to reach.

DISCUSSION QUESTIONS

Hand out the article on page 15 and ask the following:

1. How does Malcolm X define Black Nationalism? Why would this appeal to many African Americans?

2. Why does Malcolm X reject integration?

3. What is his position on the use of violence in the cause of civil rights?

4. How does he believe the government failed blacks?

5. What groups of people would support his message? What groups might feel threatened by his words?

6. Why would Malcolm X have trouble supporting Martin Luther King Jr. and vice versa?

7. Why do you think the memory of Malcolm X has been so powerful in the African-American community since his death in 1965?

Malcolm X, Press Conference,
March 12, 1964

The political philosophy of black nationalism means: we must control the politics and the politicians of our community. They must no longer take orders from outside forces. We will organize, and sweep out of office all Negro politicians who are puppets for the outside forces... .

...Whites can help us, but they can't join us. There can be no black-white unity until there is first black unity. There can be no workers' solidarity until there is first some racial solidarity. We cannot think of uniting with others, until after we have first united among ourselves... .

Concerning nonviolence: it is criminal to teach a man not to defend himself when he is the constant victim of brutal attacks. It is legal and lawful to own a shotgun or a rifle. We believe in obeying the law.

In areas where our people are the constant victims of brutality, and the government seems unable or unwilling to protect them, we should form rifle clubs that can be used to defend our lives and our property in times of emergency... . When our people are being bitten by dogs, they are within their rights to kill those dogs.

We should be peaceful, law-abiding—but the time has come for the American Negro to fight back in self-defense whenever and wherever he is being unjustly and unlawfully attacked.

If the government thinks I am wrong for saying this, then let the government start doing its job.

Isolationism vs. Internationalism, 1919–1941

Review the introductory material and the chart "Comparing Internationalists and Isolationists" on pages 124 and 125 in the Student Edition of *Threads*. Have your students discuss the reasons why America rejected "collective security" as envisioned by Woodrow Wilson in the League of Nations.

OBJECTIVES

After the class discussion on the isolationist-internationalist struggle and reading Gerald P. Nye's "Is Neutrality Possible for America?" which follows, students will be able to:

1. outline the basic beliefs of the noninterventionists (isolationists) in the 1920s and 1930s;

2. evaluate the "isolationist impulse" as the most realistic policy for America in the world in the 1930s;

3. explain why alternatives to the isolationists' position were not effectively presented in the 1930s;

4. analyze how America's World War I experiences formed the foundation for the isolationists' rationale of the 1920s and 1930s.

DISCUSSION QUESTIONS

Hand out the article on page 17 and ask the following:

1. What were the major ideas in the noninterventionists' (isolationists') arguments in the 1930s?

2. How did the events of 1914–1917 affect American isolationists' thinking in the 1930s?

3. Why did the isolationists reject collective security between the wars?

4. What anticolonial arguments did the isolationists make?

5. Why was it difficult to counter the isolationists' position in the 1930s?

6. Did President Roosevelt handle American foreign policy effectively in the 1930s? Defend your answer.

Is Neutrality Possible for America?

No one is more jealously interested in my country's maintaining adequate national defense than I am. But I am sick of things that are being done in the name of national defense. …

…But there is still another side of this outlay for war preparedness and conduct of war. Dr. Nicholas Murray Butler has made an inventory of what we could do for mankind if we had the money today. Every city of approximately 20,000 people in those countries [in western Europe] could have a two million dollar hospital, a three million dollar library, and a ten million dollar university. With part of the balance invested at five per cent, we could pay salaries of a thousand dollars apiece to 125,000 teachers and 125,000 nurses.

The serious danger to our peace, to say nothing about our standards of common honor and decency, is so obvious that a way out of the bog in which we find ourselves must be found. A policy of strict neutrality, to become mandatory as soon as the war infection manifests itself, appears to be such a way of escape. The advantages of such mandatory legislation are easily apparent. It is simply the law of the land, a law familiar to every foreign power. Nations intent upon war are given notice and may weigh for themselves the effect of such a policy upon their ability to buy arms and other war supplies in our markets. These are very definite advantages which cannot be lightly dismissed. To such a mandatory embargo against the shipment of munitions was added, specifically for our own protection against involvement in war, the so-called cash and carry provision.

The truth is that unless a halt is called upon war preparations that are not for defense and upon the enactment of laws for the complete mobilization of our civil organization in wartime, America will succumb to war psychology and will be drawn inevitably into actual conflict. Neutrality, aided by the natural advantages of our physical so-called isolation, or neutrality, happily in co-operation with other nations, if that can be safely accomplished, appears to be the solution.

When we are asked to underwrite a campaign for collective security, it is plain that we are not being invited to assist in the defense of powers, or to co-operate with powers that can properly be called democratic. The defense of the British and French empires, were we to lend ourselves to a policy of collective security with those countries, would involve the continued subjugation of hundreds of millions of black and brown peoples among whom the spirit of revolt is already manifest.

For better or worse, we are part of a world order, and it is always possible that challenges may come which we cannot ignore and which will take us as a co-operator into another world war. But let us refrain from writing the ticket of procedure even before we know who our allies are to be, what the cause is to be, what the jeopardy is going to be, what the cost is going to be, and, above all, what the chances [are] of winning the cause for which we may be willing to fight.

Containment, 1945–1975

R eview the introductory materials and the chart "Containment Approaches, 1945-1975" on pages 136 and 137 in the Student Edition of *Threads*. Have your students discuss the pros and cons of the policy of containment in protecting the security of the United States and preserving world peace during the Cold War.

OBJECTIVES

After the class discussion on containment and reading the excerpts from National Security Council Paper 68 (NSC–68), which follows, students will be able to:

1. outline the basic assumption of America's containment policy;

2. trace the evolution of containment from 1945–1951;

3. evaluate the efficacy of containment in preserving world peace;

4. assess America's understanding of Soviet intentions and capabilities during the Cold War.

DISCUSSION QUESTIONS

Hand out the article on pages 19 and ask the following:

1. According to NSC–68, what was at stake in the Cold War?

2. In the view of NSC–68, what were the Soviet Union's motivations and goals in the Cold War?

3. In retrospect, do you think this view of the Soviet Union was accurate?

4. How do the authors of NSC–68 frame the conflict in the Cold War? (That is, what forces does it suggest were in combat?) Does this seem overblown?

5. Compare the ideas and the outlook expressed in NSC–68 with the Truman Doctrine. How are they similar and different? What does this tell you about the evolution of containment?

6. What actions do the authors of NSC–68 want the United States to take?

7. What impact on American society do you think the recommendations of NSC–68 had?

National Security Council Paper 68

The issues that face us are momentous, involving the fulfillment or destruction not [only] of this Republic but of civilization itself. They are issues which will not await our deliberations. With conscience and resolution this Government and the people it represents must now take new and fateful decisions ... The fundamental design of those who control the Soviet Union and the international communist movement is to retain and solidify their absolute power, first in the Soviet Union and second in the areas now under their control. In the minds of the Soviet leaders, however, achievement of this design requires the dynamic of their authority and the ultimate elimination of any effective opposition to their authority.

The design, therefore, calls for the complete subversion or forcible destruction of the machinery of government and structure of society in the countries of the non-Soviet world and their replacement by an apparatus and structure subservient to and controlled from the Kremlin. To that end Soviet efforts are now directed toward domination of the Eurasian land mass ...

The Kremlin regards the United States as the only major threat to the achievement of its fundamental design. There is a basic conflict between the idea of freedom under a government of laws, and the idea of slavery under the grim oligarchy of the Kremlin ... The implacable purpose of the slave state to eliminate the challenge of freedom has placed the two great powers at opposite poles ...

This broad intention embraces two subsidiary policies. One is a policy which we would probably pursue even if there were no Soviet threat. It is a policy of attempting to develop a healthy international community. The other is the policy of "containing" the Soviet system ...

... The frustration of the Kremlin design requires the free world to develop a successfully functioning political and economic system and a vigorous political offensive against the Soviet Union. These, in turn, require an adequate military shield under which they can develop. It is necessary to have the military power to deter, if possible, Soviet expansion, and to defeat, if necessary, aggressive Soviet or Soviet-directed actions of a limited or total character. The potential strength of the free world is great; its ability to develop these military capabilities and its will to resist Soviet expansion will be determined by the wisdom and will with which it undertakes to meet its political and economic problems.... .

In summary, we must, by means of rapid and sustained build-up of the political, economic and military strength of the free world, and by means of an affirmative program intended to wrest the initiative from the Soviet Union, confront it with convincing evidence of the determination and ability of the free world to frustrate the Kremlin design of a world dominated by its will.... . The whole success of the proposed program hangs ultimately on recognition by this Government, the American people, and all free people, that the cold war is in fact a war in which the survival of the free world is at stake.

Lesson Plan 34

Failure of Containment— The Vietnam War

Review the introductory material and the chart "Overview of the Vietnam War" on pages 140 and 141 in the Student Edition of Threads. Have your students identify two or three turning points in the war where the United States might have avoided being pulled into the quagmire that the war became. Students should defend their choices.

OBJECTIVES

After the class discussion the Vietnam War and America's failure at containment, and reading Eisenhower's letter to Ngo Dinh Diem which follows, students will be able to:

1. identify the motivation that propelled American involvement in Vietnam;

2. analyze the assumptions about Communism that America held in the 1950s;

3. list the mistakes the United States made as it became involved in the Vietnam War;

4. assess the role of the Eisenhower administration on U. S. involvement in Vietnam.

DISCUSSION QUESTIONS

Hand out the article on page 21 and ask the following:

1. What evidence is there in Eisenhower's letter that the United States might encourage Diem not to follow the Geneva agreement?

2. Why did Eisenhower offer to assist Diem's government?

3. What was Eisenhower's goal in Vietnam? Why did this goal prove unattainable for the United States?

4. What did Eisenhower require of Diem's government in return for aid?

5. Why was this requirement never met, and how was it the heart of the problem for the United States in Vietnam?

6. What assumption does Eisenhower make about the threat that Diem's government faced?

7. To what extent did the ideas outlined in Eisenhower's letter lead to America's ultimate failure in Vietnam?

Letter from President Eisenhower
to Ngo Dinh Diem

DEAR MR. PRESIDENT: I have been following with great interest the course of developments in Viet-Nam, particularly since the conclusion of the conference at Geneva. The implications of the agreement concerning Viet-Nam have caused grave concern regarding the future of a country temporarily divided by an artificial military grouping, weakened by a long and exhausting war and faced with enemies without and by their subversive collaborators within.

Your recent requests for aid to assist in the formidable project of the movement of several hundred thousand loyal Vietnamese citizens away from areas which are passing under a de facto rule and political ideology which they abhor are being fulfilled. I am glad that the United States is able to assist in this humanitarian effort.

We have been exploring ways and means to permit our aid to Viet-Nam to be more effective and to make a greater contribution to the welfare and stability of the Government of Viet-Nam. I am, accordingly, instructing the American Ambassador to Viet-Nam to examine with you in your capacity, as Chief of Government, how an intelligent program of American aid given directly to your Government can serve to assist Viet-Nam in its present hour of trial, provided that your Government is prepared to give assurances as [to] the standards of performance it would be able to maintain in the event such aid were supplied.

The purpose of this offer is to assist the Government of Viet-Nam in developing and maintaining a strong, viable state, capable of resisting attempted subversion or aggression through military means. The Government of the United States expects that this aid will be met by performance on the part of the Government of Viet-Nam in undertaking needed reforms. It hopes that such aid, combined with your own continuing efforts will contribute effectively toward an independent Viet-Nam endowed with a strong government. Such a government would, I hope, be so responsive to the nationalist aspirations of its people, so enlightened in purpose and effective in performance, that it will be respected both at home and abroad and discourage any who might wish to impose a foreign ideology on your free people.

Sincerely,

Dwight Eisenhower

Answers & Explanations for the
Source Activities

The following suggested answers are just that—suggestions. These suggestions, however, are a good starting point for you and your students to discuss and build upon as a class. They are offered as a roadmap to begin to answer the exercises connected to the sources that accompany each lesson in *Threads of History*. You will want to add your own details and interpretations to these answers to enhance meaning, context, and to meet the specific needs of your individual students.

Wherever possible each suggested answer has been linked to one of the seven thematic Learning Objectives found in the new APUSH course framework. The seven objectives by theme are:

- American and National Identity (**NAT**) with 4 sub objectives of student analysis and explanation

- Work, Exchange, and Technology (**WXT**) with 3 sub-objectives

- Migration and Settlement (**MIG**) with 2 sub-objectives

- Politics and Power (**POL**) with 3 sub-objectives

- America in the World (**WOR**) with 2 sub-objectives

- Geography and the Environment (**GEO**) with 1 sub-objective

- Culture and Society (**CUL**) with 4 sub-objectives

In some cases, the question addresses more than one objective.

In addition, most of the suggested responses have been connected to one of the following nine categories of Historical Thinking Skills, also found in the new APUSH course framework:

- Historical Causation

- Patterns of Continuity and Change over Time

- Periodization

- Comparison

- Contextualization

- Historical Argumentation

- Appropriate Use of Relevant Historical Evidence

- Interpretation

- Synthesis

Lesson 1: Historical Periods

Multiple-Choice

1. The best answer is (B). As part of the deal to make Rutherford Hayes president, the last federal troops were withdrawn from the South. This symbolic gesture sent a message that Reconstruction was over and removed the last pressures on the South to abide by the Radical Republican program that had been assembled after the Civil War. (Pol-3, Use of Relevant Historical Evidence)

2. The best answer is (A). With three states (Florida, South Carolina, and Louisiana) in dispute in the election, neither candidate had a majority in the Electoral College. All the disputed votes were given to Hayes in return for the Republicans' agreement to pull the troops from the South. The Compromise marked the end of Reconstruction. (Pol-3, Periodization)

Short-Answer

a. Answers will vary. The Freedmen suffered greatly as a result of the election. The Redeemers were ex-Confederates who reasserted themselves when the troops were withdrawn and they proceeded to implement a Jim Crow system throughout the South. The Radical Republicans were in decline with less and less influence. The election punctuated their retreat. (Pol-3, Periodization, Use of Relevant Historical Evidence)

b. Answers will vary. (NAT-4, Use of Relevant Historical Evidence)

c. Answers will vary. Students might explain the various Supreme Court Cases from the Slaughterhouse Cases to *Plessy v. Ferguson*. They might mention the two depressions of 1873 and 1893 as diverting attention away from civil rights. And they might mention the cultural impact of Thomas Dixon's books, which depicted the Ku Klux Klan in a heroic way and demeaned African Americans. (POL-1, Historical Argumentation)

Lesson 2: Famous Rebellions

Multiple-Choice

1. The best answer is (A). Shays's Rebellion showed that the emphasis on liberty and freedom expressed during the Revolution needed to be modified in the 1780s when liberty seemed to become license. A central government authority, which had been an anathema to revolutionaries, now seemed necessary. (POL-1, Use of Relevant Historical Evidence)

2. The best answer is (D). The farmers of western Pennsylvania refused to pay their whiskey tax. The new government under Washington exercised "energy" by collecting the tax by force. Washington's forceful suppression of the protest caused controversy in his Cabinet (Jefferson) and in the nation. (POL-2, Historical Causation)

Short-Answer

a. Answers will vary. Shays's Rebellion shook up Washington's political thinking because he feared the nation was coming apart. He accepted more power in a central government, a revision of the Articles of Confederation, and a willingness to attend the Constitutional

Convention. His attendance at the meeting gave it importance and legitimacy in the eyes of many colonial citizens. (POL-2, Patterns of Continuity and Change over Time)

b. Answers will vary. Students might explain: that acceptance of suppression of dissent ran counter to the liberty achieved by the revolutionary leaders such as Washington; that the Articles overall provided a government supported by a majority of Americans and that they need only to be slightly changed; that attendance in Philadelphia raised questions about the motives and agenda of the participants who might replace the Articles with an oppressive government along the lines of England's. (POL-2, Historical Causation)

Lesson 3: Religious Development, 1619–1740

Multiple-Choice

1. The best answer is (C). The Puritans created a theocracy in Massachusetts. They believed the church and state should be united and that the church should govern the colonies as the civil authority. (CUL-1, Use of Relevant Historical Evidence)

2. The best answer is (B). When the Constitution was written, the authors made sure that there were no religious tests for office and that the church and state were separated. The First Amendment to the Constitution addressed this concern. (CUL-1, Historical Causation)

Short-Answer

a. Answers will vary. The platform stated that not everyone would be accepted in church; and that the church (civil authority) would enforce the rules of the colony. (CUL-1, Use of Relevant Historical Evidence)

b. Answers will vary. (CUL-1, Use of Relevant Historical Evidence)

c. The Puritans were known for their exclusivity, their intolerance, and their harsh suppression of dissent and "misbehavior." (NAT-1, Historical Causation)

Lesson 4: Presidents of the United States, 1789–2001

Multiple-Choice

1. The best answer is (C). Jefferson's statement that "We are all Republicans, we are all Federalists" was a call for national unity and bi-partisanship. He hoped to put the divisiveness of the past over foreign and domestic issues behind the nation. He did not succeed. (POL-1, Use of Relevant Historical Evidence)

2. The best answer is (B). Jefferson was referring to the partisan debate that surrounded the rights of the people to protest taxes (Whiskey Rebellion) and to express their freedom of speech, which the Sedition Act severely restricted. Both actions were challenged by the Republicans, but they were unable to stop the Federalist majority from implementing them in the mid and late 1790s. (POL-1, Comparison)

Short-Answer

a. Jefferson called on the nation to come together as one people and accept the verdict of the election. The people had spoken and must be obeyed. He also encouraged tolerance for legal dissent. He believed that protesters should be heard until they came to realize the errors of the views. (POL-1, Historical Causation)

b. Answers will vary. Students might note Jefferson's Judiciary Act of 1801, which challenged various judges, support for the Impeachment of Samuel Chase, the Purchase of Louisiana, and then enacted the Embargo Act of 1807. All actions occurred over the protest and opposition of the Federalists. (POL-1, Use of Relevant Historical Evidence)

c. Jefferson showed the ability to lead the nation in the peaceful transfer of power from one political group to another. His measured response gave hope that America's republican experiment could work and survive. (POL-1, Use of Relevant Historical Evidence)

Lesson 5: The First and Second Great Awakenings

Multiple-Choice

1. The best answer is (C). Religious groups promoted social and economic agendas during many periods in the 20th century. For example, during the Progressive Era, the Social Gospel movement was active in encouraging government action to promote social justice. In the 1920s, evangelicals, while conservative in their beliefs, embraced certain policies such as Prohibition. In the 1930s, Father Charles Coughlin, a Catholic priest, endorsed free silver and criticized the New Deal for its lack of attention to the poor. And in the 1950s and 1960s, Martin Luther King used religion as a basis for civil rights reforms. (CUL-1, Patterns of Continuity and Change over Time)

2. The best answer is (D). Women were very active in the Second Great Awakening. Drawing inspiration from the religious ideas of salvation for themselves and others, they joined the abolitionist movement and sought equal rights for all people. These actions challenged the conventional thinking (cult of domesticity) of the era. (CUL-1, Historical Causation)

Short-Answer

a. Answers will vary. Women took an active role in many aspects of the Second Great Awakening. These actions challenged the cult of domesticity as women took on duties outside of their normal sphere (the home). Clergy became active in the reforms of abolitionist and temperance and used their influence to change societal policies. They often traveled outside of their churches to spread the word of God and change. Male participants in the Second Great Awakening were challenged to broaden the concept of democracy to include the disadvantages and the oppressed. (NAT-1, CUL-1, Historical Causation)

b. Answers will vary. Students might explain the general spirit of reform in the era. They might mention the rise of abolition and other movements. They might also credit reformers such as Charles Finney and William Garrison with creating a spirit of reform. Also the Panic of 1837 shook up the country. (NAT-1, Historical Causation)

c. Answers will vary. Many political and social conservatives pushed back against the various reforms and reformers. Andrew Jackson and Catherine Beecher were not sympathetic to many of the reformers with abolitionists and women's suffrage supporters under great stress. (NAT-1, Historical Causation)

Lesson 6: Coming of the American Revolution

Multiple-Choice

1. The best answer is (D). The Sons of Liberty were opposed to the ideas of remaining in the Empire. They could not see any real advantage for continuing with the colonial relationship that seemed to be enslaving the Americans. (NAT-1, Use of Relevant Historical Evidence)

2. The best answer is (A). After the Revolution, the Loyalists tried to get compensation for the property that they abandoned when tens of thousands Tories left America for England and Canada. The British occupied forts on American soil until the mid 1790s when the Jay Treaty resolved most of the disputes. (NAT-1, Contextualization)

Short-Answer

a. Answers will vary. The Stamp Act gave the colonists a new sense of unity as 9 of 13 colonies joined in New York to protest the Stamp Act. The Boston Massacre helped heightened the colonial outrage against Great Britain as five colonials were shot and killed in Boston. It was another stepping stone to an emerging national unity. The Tea Party promoted a final unification of the colonies as 12 of 13 met in Philadelphia to decide how to help Massachusetts resist the Intolerable Acts.
(NAT-1, Use of Relevant Historical Evidence)

b. Answers will vary. (NAT-1, Use of Relevant Historical Evidence)

c. Answers will vary. Students might explain that the British:

   (1) sent troops to colonies

   (2) offered colonists representation in Parliament

   (3) proposed the concept of virtual representation

   (4) repealed the Stamp Act, Townshend Acts

   (5) reminded colonists that Parliament was superior to colonial assemblies

   (6) appealed to colonists' loyalty as Englishmen abroad.

   (NAT-1, Use of Relevant Historical Evidence)

Lesson 7: The National Banks

Multiple-Choice

1. The best answer is (A). After the Civil War, the issue of the type and amount of currency in circulation dominated the economic and political debate. Farmers wanted silver and/or paper money added to the gold in circulation to inflate the money supply and to aid debtors. The issue was comparable to the pre-Civil War debate over the National Bank. Both controversies revolved around the advantages economic policies gave to the rich and the elites in society and to wealthy easterners in particular. (POL-3, Continuity and Change)

2. The best answer is (B). Alexander Hamilton's financial plan was seen as benefiting the elite in society. Similar charges were made against both the First and Second National Banks. Also his plan called for an expansion of the central government's economic reach in a fashion that was similar to the increased governmental role that went along with the creation of the National Banks. (POL-3, Continuity and Change)

Short-Answer

a. Answers will vary. Jackson's constituents (western and southern farmers) supported the veto of the Bank, but its elimination had an adverse impact on the American economy. The Specie Circular curtailed land speculation by requiring land purchases to be made in gold or silver. This requirement tamed inflation, but it helped to cause the Panic of 1837. The pet banks made credit more available, especially in the South and the West, but they also made risky investments that generated speculation and inflation. (POL-3, Use of Relevant Historical Evidence)

b. Jackson attempted to reduce the federal government's reach in the economy. He sought to curtail the growth of federal power that occurred after the War of 1812 as the government increased the tariff; reconstituted the National Bank; and embarked on an expanded internal improvements program. (POL-3, Use of Relevant Historical Evidence)

c. Answers will vary. Students might explain opposition to both Banks revolved around:

   (1) the government had no business in the Banking industry;

   (2) the Bank was a tool of the rich;

   (3) the Bank favored one class of Americans over another;

   (4) general tax receipts were used to promote a private business;

   (5) the Bank was foreign owned.

   (POL-3, Continuity and Change)

Lesson 8: *Liberal* and *Conservative* in the United States, 1790–1940

Multiple-Choice

1. The best answer is (A). The members of the Social Gospel movement believe the churches should encourage the government to take responsibility to defend people's welfare and opportunities. Roosevelt supported this concept as he believed government regulation of trusts (monopolies) would provide a "Square Deal" for the less powerful in society and giving them a better chance to succeed in life.
    (POL-2, Use of Relevant Historical Evidence)

2. The best answer is (C). The progressives, led by presidents Theodore Roosevelt, William Taft, and Woodrow Wilson used the Sherman Anti-Trust Act over two hundred times to reign in the power of large corporations and trusts. While never attempting to take over the businesses or to restore old-fashion competition, the progressives hoped to regulate corporations and protect the public interest. (POL-2, Historical Causation)

Short-Answer

a. Answers will vary. Each of the three groups called on the government to alleviate the suffering of the poor. The Populist Party with its Omaha Platform probably had the greatest influence on the Progressive Movement among the three. The Greenback Labor Party called for the government to reform the currency and to help debtors. And the Women's Christian Temperance Union anticipated the Prohibition movement with their drive to restrict the use of alcohol. (Some historians view the 18th Amendment as one of the last gasps of progressive reform.)
    (POL-2, Historical Causation, Continuity/ Change)

b. Answers will vary. (POL-2, Historical Causation)

c. Answers will vary. Students might explain that both the years 1901–1917 and 1933–1941 shared some common characteristics:

    (1) strong executive leadership in the White House;

    (2) followed an era of reduced government activities;

    (3) saw a popular belief that businesses had grown too large and were somewhat abusive to the general welfare;

    (4) followed economic downturns (Depressions of 1893–1897 and 1929–1933)

    (POL-3, Historical Causation)

Lesson 9: *Liberal* and *Conservative* in the United States, 1940–1985

Multiple-Choice

1. The best answer is (C). The conservative movement spearheaded by Barry Goldwater believed that the nation became weak after the debacle of Vietnam. America's retreat in the 1970s led many to believe American security and place in the world had slipped. The Reagan presidency from 1981-1989 reversed this trend with expansion of military spending and a more confrontational approach to the Soviet Union. (POL-1, Historical Causation)

2. The best answer is (D). The conservative movement, especially in the 1920s, sought to lessen the role of government in society as it reacted to the progressive reforms of the early 20th century. The policies of Harding and Coolidge in particular cut regulations and taxation from the pre- Great War era. (POL-1, Continuity/Change)

Short-Answer

a. Answers will vary. Goldwater suggested the following in his speech: American foreign policy was weak and adrift in the mid-1960s; the federal government did not promote job growth, rather it expanded its bureaucracy and stifled economic growth; freedom was endangered by the current administration's attempts to cooperate with the communists. (POL-1, Continuity/Change)

b. Answers will vary. Students might explain:

    (1) the United States had setbacks in fighting Communism (Castro in Cuba);

    (2) the U-2 episode ruined peaceful coexistence and the Cold War had deepened;

    (3) the U.S. and Soviet Union signed a Nuclear Test Ban Treaty, which many saw as favorable to the U.S.S.R.;

    (4) the Soviets made inroads in the Middle East, Africa, and space.

    (POL-1, Use of Relevant Historical Evidence)

Lesson 10: Political Parties in the Nineteenth Century

Multiple-Choice

1. The best answer is (D). Adams called for the government to expand its role in society. His activism was based on the elastic clause that called on Congress to take "necessary and proper" actions (in Adams' thinking) and make improvements in agriculture, commerce, and advancements in the arts. Adams proposed this expansion, but the Jacksonians blocked his endeavors. (POL-1, Continuity/ Change)

2. The best answer is (C). The Whig Party grew from the National Republicans, which Adams briefly headed. The Whigs called for the government to be beneficent and paternal in its policies. The party supported building roads, canals, and a new National Bank. The party was significant politically from 1832-1852. (POL-1, Contextualization)

Short-Answer

a. Answers will vary. The end of the War of 1812 marked a new era of government activism, which Adams supports in the passage. The government raised the tariff, re-chartered the Bank, and began a limited program of road and canal building. The American System supported internal improvements, the National Bank, and higher tariffs. The re-charter of the National Bank in 1816 supported the idea that the federal government should play an active role in the financial and economic development of the nation. (POL-1, Historical Causation)

b. Answers will vary. The rise of Jacksonian democracy after the election of 1824 challenged the agenda of the National Republicans and later the Whigs as they tried to expand the power of the federal government. Jackson's veto of the Maysville Road and the National Bank demonstrated his commitment to reducing the power of the government. Martin Van Buren continued Jackson's policies in his term from 1837-1841. (POL-2, Use of Relevant Historical Evidence)

Lesson 11: Third Parties in United States History

Multiple-Choice

1. The best answer is (D). The cartoon depicts the attempt by the Grange to regulate railroads. The railroads had a monopoly in many parts of the West and abused farmers with rates that were unfair and capricious. The farmers hoped to change the dominance of railroads through government regulation of rates and policies. (WXT-2, Historical Causation)

2. The best answer is (A). The Grange and other farmers' organizations hoped to reverse the declining economic and political power of agrarian interests after the Civil War. Although the absolute numbers of farmers increased during these years, the percentage of farmers in the workforce declined. In addition, farm prices tumbled by 1/3 from 1868–1896. (WXT-2, Continuity/Change)

Short-Answer

a. Answers will vary. The farmers needed to become active and defend themselves against railroad abuses. Farm organizations attempted to unite farmers and to fight the railroads. The railroad executives disliked agrarian groups attempting to reduce their profits and interfering with their consolidation of power in the west. Passengers on the train, representing the general public, did not want their lives disrupted by protests nor did they support farmers' attempt to raise food prices. (WXT-2, Use of Relevant Historical Evidence)

b. Answers will vary. (WXT-2, Use of Relevant Historical Evidence)

c. Answers will vary. Students might explain the Grange Laws, the creation of the Interstate Commerce Commission, the Greenback Labor Party, and the Populists. All of which tried to reign in the power of the railroads before the turn of the century.
(WXT-2, Use of Relevant Historical Evidence)

Lesson 12: Freedom of the Seas and Wars in Europe

Multiple-Choice

1. The best answer is (B). In his Farewell Address, Washington called for the United States to avoid "entangling alliances" in Europe. When the nation tried to stay out of the conflict between England and France in the 1790s and early 1800s, both nations attacked our ships. Great Britain, however, also began to impress our sailors. This slap at our honor and trade eventually led to war in 1812. (WOR-1, Historical Causation)

2. The best answer is (C). New England shippers, while the victims of much of England's trade interdiction and loss of seamen, still were realizing great profits. As the most important neutral trading partner, the New Englanders (and the United States in general) saw their shipping interests flourish during the European conflict. With war, all trade ceased between England and depression replaced prosperity in the Northeast.
(WXT-2, Use of Relevant Historical Evidence)

Short-Answer

a. Answers will vary. The Embargo Act of 1807 was a total stoppage of trade with all countries. The act took American shipping off the seas until American rights on the seas were recognized by England and France. The Non Intercourse Act was a partial embargo with the United States trading with all countries except England and France. Macon Bill No. 2 was another partial embargo with a different wrinkle. It said the United States would trade with all countries, but if either Great Britain or France agreed to stop interfering with our shipping, America would stop trading with that countries' enemy. All three actions tried to avoid both war and submission, but war came in 1812 with England.
(NAT-1, Use of Relevant Historical Evidence)

b. Answers will vary. Students might explain:

(1) Presidents Jefferson, Madison, and Wilson all tried to avoid war;

(2) all followed Washington's advice to avoid entangling the United States in European conflicts;

(3) all used diplomacy and the threat of economic retaliation to avoid war;

(4) Madison and Wilson reluctantly asked for a declaration of war.

(WOR-1, Comparison)

Lesson 13: Compromises and the Union

Multiple-Choice

1. The best answer is (D). Calhoun spoke for the right of southerners to own slaves and to take them into the territories. He opposed the series of legislative proposals known as the Compromise of 1850. These bills included the concept of popular sovereignty, which allowed the people of a territory to decide whether to permit slavery or not. Calhoun believed slavery could not be excluded in the territories under any circumstances. (WXT-1, Continuity/Change)

2. The best answer is (A). Calhoun was a strict constructionist. He believed the South had a constitutional right to hold slaves and to expand the institution westward. He cited the Fifth Amendment as support that property (slaves included) could not be taken without just compensation or due process. He also called attention to the fugitive slave provision and the 3/5 Compromise as evidence of constitutional support of the peculiar institution. (POL-3, Use of Relevant Historical Evidence)

Short-Answer

a. Answers will vary. The 3/5 Compromise addressed the conflict over how to count slaves for taxation and representation purposes at the Constitutional Convention. Both the North and South thought it fair at the time, but later the North complained the South got an unfair advantage in Congress and in presidential elections. The Missouri Compromise provided a thirty year truce over the question of the slavery's expansion. When it was repealed in the 1850s, it set off a political firestorm. The Compromise of 1833 solved the nullification dispute of the 1830s. South Carolina refused to pay the tariff and civil war seemed possible. While the compromise restored peace, many historians viewed the dispute as a preview of the South's growing concern over an increasing intrusive government that triggered the Civil War in the 1860s. (POL-3, Use of Relevant Historical Evidence)

b. Answers will vary. (POL-3, Use of Relevant Historical Evidence)

c. Answers will vary. Students might cite the Great Compromise at the Constitutional Convention, the Compromise of 1850 or the Compromise of 1877. Each provide a political settlement that prevented a crisis. (POL-3, Use of Relevant Historical Evidence)

Lesson 14: Judicial Nationalism, 1819–1824

Multiple-Choice

1. The best answer is (C). The Jacksonians endorsed the ideas expressed in the passage that the federal government was growing too powerful and intruding on states' rights. In the 1830s, Jackson and his allies attempted to restrict the government's role in the economy by destroying the National Bank, and, at least, temporarily cutting back on federal sponsorship of internal improvements. (POL-2, Historical Causation, Contextualization)

2. The best answer is (A). The passage raised the issue of federal versus states rights. This was the core question that arose during the civil rights movement of the 1950s and 1960s. The southern states claimed they were solely responsible for their citizens' rights and welfare. (NAT-1, POL-3, Continuity/Change)

Short-Answers

a. Answers will vary. The passage expressed fears of the growth of a central government at the expense of the states. The federal government encroached on the states with its taxing power, its support of business interests, and promotion of internal improvements. (POL-1, Use of Relevant Historical Evidence)

b. The Marshall Court in the decisions of *Dartmouth College v. Woodward, McCulloch v. Maryland* and *Gibbons v. Ogden* expanded the power of the federal government and promoted business interests and commerce. The overall effect of the rulings was to extend the power of the central government into states' rights. And this was exactly the fear expressed in the passage. (POL-3, Use of Relevant Historical Evidence)

c. Answers will vary. The cases most likely to be cited are *Dred Scott v. Sandford* and *Plessy v. Ferguson*. Students might also mention The Slaughouse Cases, The Civil Rights Cases, Ex parte Milligan, Ex parte Merryman, or *U.S. v. Cruikshank*. (POL-3, Continuity/ Change)

Lesson 15: Cornerstones of United States Foreign Policy

Multiple-Choice

1. The best answer is (B). America's Imperialism in the 1890s reflected both domestic and foreign pressures to look outward. Officials at home hoped to solve the domestic and social problems that arose during the Depression of 1893 by expanded overseas. Many Americans also realized that the "race of empire" was a world-wide competition and that the United States must compete with other nations for possessions around the globe. (WOR-2, Historical Causation)

2. The best answer is (A). The cartoon reflected America's expanding interest in the Caribbean and its willingness to use force if necessary to protect the Panama Canal, and establish American hegemony in the Caribbean and South America. (WOR-2, Historical Causation)

Short-Answers

a. Answers will vary. (WOR-2, Use of Relevant Historical Evidence)

b. Answers will vary. (WOR-2, Use of Relevant Historical Evidence)

c. Answers will vary. Students might explain that in the years 1930-1965, the United States tried to reverse the Big Stick, aggressive policies of the early twentieth century and embarked on The Good Neighbor Policy in the 1930s and the Alliance for Progress in the 1960s. Both eras emphasized cooperation and some multi-lateral solutions to the hemisphere's problems. (WOR-2, Use of Relevant Historical Evidence)

Lesson 16: Expansion of the United States, 1783–1853

Multiple-Choice

1. The best answer is (C). The passage suggested that other nations were trying to influence events in Texas. The idea of European meddling in the affairs of the Western Hemisphere had been a concern going back to 1823 and the issuance of the Monroe Doctrine. (NAT-1, Continuity/ Change)

2. The best answer is (D). The passage, written in the mid-1840s, reflected the spirit of Manifest Destiny. In fact, O'Sullivan coined the phrase. A major component of this expansionistic concept was that God approved of American expansion and its acquisition of Texas. (WOR-2, Historical Causation)

Short-Answer

a. Answers will vary. Students might explain that the author was calling for the annexation of Texas. Based on America's national security needs and the Monroe Doctrine, O'Sullivan suggested that America should not allow European countries to restrict our expansion. He also noted that Texas was an independent nation that sought union with the United States. (WOR-1, Use of Relevant Historical Evidence)

b. Answers will vary. The Wilmot Provisio was added to a money bill during the early stages of the Mexican American war. It became a divisive rallying point for opponents of the expansion of slavery in the 1850s. The Compromise of 1850 was necessary when the Utah and New Mexico territories were organized. These lands were part of the Mexican Cession and raised sectional debate about the expansion of slavery. The "Slave Power" was an ephemeral construct embraced by many Northerners after the Mexican War. The conflict seemed to embolden the South as they pushed to undermine the Missouri Compromise with the Kansas-Nebraska Act, which gave further credence to the "Slave Power" existence and reach. (NAT-1, Historical Causation)

c. Answers will vary. The idea that the United States had a right to expand its territory was expressed in the late nineteenth century and early twentieth century. The nation also put military might behind the Monroe Doctrine and expanded its meaning beyond prohibiting colonization to restricting almost all European political and economic action in Latin America. (WOR-2, Continuity/ Change, Contextualization)

Lesson 17: Wars in United States History

Multiple-Choice

1. The best answer is (D). The supporters of collective security believed that stopping aggression in one country before it grew too powerful would, in the long run, be in America's national interest. Building on the pre-World War lessons against appeasing aggressor nations, and the ideals of Woodrow Wilson, they called for the United States to help other nations maintain their independence and freedom. (WOR-2, Use of Relevant Historical Evidence)

2. The best answer is (C). The United States was very active in Europe and Asia in resisting Communism by sending military aid and forces to Korea and Vietnam. In Europe, the U.S. strengthened the resistance to Communism through the North Atlantic Treaty Organization. (WOR-2, Historical Causation)

Short-Answer

a. Answers will vary. The Truman Doctrine was the first implementation of Kennan's ideas in 1947. It called for economic assistance to Greece and Turkey to block communist (U.S.S.R.) expansion into the Balkans. The Marshall Plan expanded the Truman Doctrine to most of Western Europe to help countries resist Communism. NATO was a military alliance formed in 1949 to protect Western Europe from Soviet military attack. All these actions were designed to contain the spread of Communism from 1947-1954. (WOR-2, Use of Relevant Historical Evidence)

b. Answers will vary. The Soviet Union took a series of actions from 1945-1950 that gave the United States concern and triggered the containment of Communism. Students might mention:

    (1) Soviet support of Greek rebels;

    (2) U.S.S.R. refusal to evacuate northern Iran;

    (3) a communist coup in Czechoslovakia;

    (4) the erection of an "Iron Curtain" in Eastern Europe;

    (5) Soviet support for Mao Tse Tung in the Chinese Civil War.

    (WOR-2, Use of Relevant Historical Evidence)

c. Critics of containment such as Henry Wallace called for a more conciliatory policy toward the U.S.S.R. They reminded that the Soviets were a wartime ally that had fought heroically against the Nazis, suffered enormous losses in the war, did not want to conquer the world, sought only to protect their borders, and were reacting to aggressive attempts by the U.S.A. to spread Capitalism and democracy in Eastern Europe. (WOR-2, Use of Relevant Historical Evidence)

Lesson 18: Amendments to the Constitution

Multiple-Choice

1. The best answer is (A). The Fourteenth Amendment became the foundation of much of the civil rights legislation of the 1960s and 1970s. The Court interpreted "due process and equal protection" to justify expanding social justices for many groups including women and African Americans. (NAT-2, POL-1, Continuity/Change)

2. The best answer is (B). The Fourteenth Amendment was a direct response to the Dred Scott decision of 1857. This infamous ruling denied citizenship to all African Americans, both free and enslaved. The amendment clearly defined citizenship and made the federal government ultimately responsible of protecting people's rights within the various states. (POL-1, Historical Causation)

Short-Answer

a. Answers will vary depending on the amendments selected.

b. Answers will vary depending on the amendments selected.

Lesson 19: Utopian Societies in the 1830s and 1840s

Multiple-Choice

1. The best answer is (A). The communes of the 1960s were an attempt by "Hippies" and the counter culture to drop out of the competitive, capitalistic society that had grown up after World War II in the United States. Like the members of the utopian societies of the nineteenth century, these young people rejected traditional social, political, and economic ideas and tried to create living arrangements that emphasized individual freedom and cooperation rather than aggressive competition with each other. (NAT-1, Continuity/Change)

2. The best answer is (B). The utopian societies reflected deeply held views that society should emphasize the principles of individualism and freedom. Part of the difficulty in maintaining these various experiments was that there tended to be too much freedom in the community and too little focused direction in making a living. (POL-1, Historical Causation)

Short-Answer

a. Answers will vary. The Book of Mormon, which promoted a singular religion, would fly in the face of Brook Farm's promotion of religious freedom and diversity. The Wealth of Nations, which promoted unbridled capitalism, would not fit the philosophy of Brook Farm's collective, cooperative economic model. Thoughts on Female Education, which

called for a specific educational experience for women that was distinct from men, would run counter to Brook Farm's support of gender equality.
(CUL-1, Use of Relevant Historical Evidence)

b. Answers will vary. With its support of freedom of religion, gender equality, direct democracy, and a benevolent form of socialism in economics, Brook Farm represented a stark alternative to the values and institutions of mainstream society. (CUL-1, Use of Relevant Historical Evidence)

c. Answers will vary. The growing Market Revolution that developed after the War of 1812 saw the growth of more manufacturing and commerce in the United States. Often these developments came at enormous social and economic costs. The Panic of 1837 made many people question the capitalist system of lassiez-faire and rampant competition. Also widespread poverty among immigrates troubled many Americans. (WXT-2, Historical Causation, Use of Relevant Historical Evidence)

Lesson 20: Expanding Democracy— The Abolitionist Movement

Multiple-Choice

1. The best answer is (A). The abolitionists sought to expand freedom for all people by forming newspapers such as The Liberator and The North Star. They also created organizations such as the American Anti-Slavery society that traveled around and made speeches against slavery in the North. (POL-2, Use of Relevant Historical Evidence)

2. The best answer is (C). The abolitionists drew heavily from the spiritual and intellectual messages of the Second Great Awakening, which advocated the ideal that people, should strive not only for personal salvation, but also work to achieve social justice in society at large. (POL-2, Historical Causation)

Short-Answer

a. Answers will vary. John Calhoun opposed the idea that equality for all Americans was a God given right. His racism was deeply felt and widely shared in the South. David Walker opposed Garrison non-violent approach to abolition. He believed Blacks should take direct action to gain their freedom even to the point of rebellion. Lewis Tappan opposed Garrison's moral approach to abolition. He also opposed his position attacking the Constitution and the churches. (POL-2, Use of Relevant Historical Evidence)

b. Answers will vary. (POL-2, Use of Relevant Historical Evidence)

c. Answers will vary. Students might explain that both time periods had religious developments that supported reform (The Second Great Awakening in the 1830s/1840s and Martin Luther King's church based movement in the 1950s); both eras had strong leaders (William Lloyd Garrison, Frederick Douglass, Abraham Lincoln, Martin Luther King Jr., Earl Warren, Lyndon Johnson); and both the 1840s and 1960s were a time when the reform spirit was abroad in the nation (women's movement, temperance in 1840s, protest against Vietnam, drive for gender equality, civil rights in the 1960s).
(POL-2, Comparison, Use of Relevant Historical Evidence)

Lesson 21: Women's Movement during the Nineteenth Century

Multiple-Choice

1. The best answer is (D). The cartoon depicted the social forces working against women (references to women's apparel and the voting booth), and the legal barriers symbolized by the policeman and the issue of public policy (taxes). This combination represented a strong barrier to women achieving equal rights from 1840–1920.
    (NAT-1, Use of Relevant Historical Evidence)

2. The best answer (C). The quest for women's voting rights was similar to women's drive to liberalize the divorce laws in the 1840s and 1850s. Divorce laws greatly limited women's power in society and their change empowered women just as the right to vote would eventually achieve. (POL-2, Continuity/Change)

Short-Answer

a. Answers will vary. Susan B. Anthony would challenge the point of view. She was a strong advocate for women's suffrage regardless of the societal barriers. Frederick Douglass would have mixed feelings about women voting. He had strongly supported the 15th Amendment and wanted women to postpone their drive for suffrage until black men were secure in the voting booth. Catherine Beecher did not support suffrage for women. She was a proponent of the "cult of true womanhood" in the 19th century.
    (POL-2, Use of Relevant Historical Evidence)

b. Answers will vary. (NAT-1, Use of Relevant Historical Evidence)

c. Answers will vary. Students might explain that passage of the 19th Amendment, the League of Women Voters, Title X of the Civil Rights Act of 1964, *Roe v. Wade*, *The Feminine Mystique*, and the formation of the National Organization of Women all helped to expand women's social and political rights in the twentieth century.
    (NAT-1, Contextualization, Continuity/Change)

Lesson 22: Major Treaties in United States History

Multiple-Choice

1. The best answer is (C). The cartoon depicted Henry Cabot Lodge, a leading reservationist, shepherding the Treaty of Versailles from the operating room where his amendments had preserved, but also altered, membership in the League of Nations.
    (WOR-2, Use of Relevant Historical Evidence)

2. The best answer is (B). After the rejection of the treaty, the United States embarked on a period of retreat from political and military connections with Europe. While maintaining commercial relationships and joining in disarmament agreements, the United States did

not join either the League of Nations or the World Court. These isolationist tendencies reached their apex in the mid 1930s with enactment of the Neutrality Acts.
(WOR-2, Historical Causation)

Short-Answer

a. Answers will vary. Henry Cabot Lodge approved of the point of view in the cartoon. While supporting much of the Treaty of Versailles and the League of Nations, he led the group that demanded changes (reservations) to the document and the organization. As the leader of the irreconcilables, William Borah wanted the treaty slaughtered (rejected) rather than modified. Woodrow Wilson opposed the point of view of the cartoon. He wanted the treaty and League approved in the same form with which he negotiated it in Paris. He opposed all changes (reservations) proposed by Lodge.
(WOR-2, Historical Argumentation)

b. Answers will vary. (WOR-2, Historical Argumentation)

c. Answers will vary. The rise of Fascism in Germany, Italy and Japan in the 1930s all called into question America's refusal to take an active role in the League of Nations and international political affairs. The Lodge reservations, which doomed the Treaty of Versailles, curtailed America's role in Europe and Asia, and set a tone that lingered into the late 1930s. (WOR-2, Contextualization, Continuity/Change)

Lesson 23: Reconstruction of the South

Multiple-Choice

1. The best answer is (A). The Radical Republicans, led by Thaddeus Stevens, called upon Congress to guarantee citizenship rights to African Americans and, for Black men, the right to vote. These rights were established and protected by the 14th and 15th Amendments. (NAT-2, Historical Causation)

2. The best answer is (B). The foundation of the Radical Republican program was the promises of unalienable rights to life, liberty and the pursuit of happiness made in the Declaration of Independence to all men. The passage noted that all men had a soul, and were entitled to "justice, honesty and fair play."
(NAT-1, Historical Causation, Continuity/Change)

Short-Answer

a. Answers will vary. The Freemen's Bureau extended assistance to former slaves. It provided education, welfare, and briefly land to Freedmen. The Bureau performed tasks that the South opposed. The 14th Amendment gave citizenship to African Americans and made it clear that if states did not protect their citizens, the federal government had the right to step in and offer protection to Blacks. The 15th Amendment gave Black men the right to vote. In the short run, this allowed the election of African Americans to political offices throughout the South. (POL-3, Contextualization)

b. Answers will vary. Students might explain states' rights, racism, lingering resentments from the Civil War, and strict constructionist views of the Constitution.

c. Answers will vary. Students might explain the rise of the Ku Klux Klan, the use of poll taxes and grandfather clauses to restrict voting, the creation of Jim Crow laws, and the court's reduction of the reach of the Fourteenth Amendment. (Pol-3, Historical Causation)

Lesson 24: Judicial Betrayal— The Road to *Plessy v. Ferguson*

Multiple-Choice

1. The best answer is (C). The Civil Rights cases reinforced the idea that the states were responsible for day-to-day protections of their citizens. The cases reduced the reach of the 14th Amendment and left African Americans at the mercy of their home state. This contributed to attacks such as lynching against blacks. (NAT-2, Historical Causation)

2. The best answer is (B). The abolitionists advocated the ending of slavery and wanted an active federal effort to protect basic rights and safety for all people in the United States. The ruling narrowed the range of action the federal government could undertake under the 14th Amendment and left the protection of African American rights in the hands of indifferent and often hostile state governments in the South. (NAT-2, Contextualization, Use of Relevant Historical Evidence)

Short-Answer

a. Answers will vary. J. Strom Thurmond, the leader of the States' Right Party (Dixiecrats) in the late 1940s, would favor the decision because it gave states the power to block federal interference in disputes between whites and blacks. Thurgood Marshall, a lawyer for the National Association for the Advancement of Colored People (NAACP), would oppose the ruling because he looked to the federal government to override the states, and to end the Jim Crow system in America. W.E.B. DuBois, a leading spokesman for civil rights, would oppose the ruling because it tightened the Jim Crow system that he and others spent their lives trying to dismantle. (NAT-2, Use of Relevant Historical Evidence)

b. Answers will vary. (NAT-2, Use of Relevant Historical Evidence)

c. Answers will vary. Students mostly likely would cite *Brown v. Board of Education*, but they might offer *McLaurin v. Oklahoma State Regents* (1950), which said a student could not be segregated within a classroom and/or *Sweatt v. Painter* (1950), which ruled that a law school created hastily for blacks did not meet the equality requirement of "separate but equal." (NAT-2, Use of Relevant Historical Evidence)

Lesson 25: Monetary Policy—
Gold vs. Silver, 1862–1900

Multiple-Choice

1. The best answer is (D). The government's decisions after the Civil War to take greenbacks out of circulation and to stop coining silver dollars reduced the amount of currency in circulation. Farmers and debtors were certain that these actions were the root cause of their economic distress.
   (WXT-2, Use of Relevant Historical Evidence, Historical Causation)

2. The best answer is (B). The debate over currency in the late nineteenth century paralleled the earlier struggle over banking during Jackson's presidency. In both cases, the conflict was framed as a struggle between rich and poor. Also in both eras, agrarian interest struggled with mercantile groups for economic control and advantage.
   (POL-3, Continuity/Change)

Short-Answer

a. Answers will vary. William Jennings Bryan, an advocate for free sliver, would agree with the ideas of expanding the money supply by coining silver at a rate of 16 to 1. James B. Weaver, a support of both greenback dollars and later silver would also support the ideas expressed by Harvey. Grover Cleveland, a Gold Democrat, would oppose the ideas in the passage. He supported gold as the only standard currency.
   (WXT-2, Use of Relevant Historical Evidence)

b. Answers will vary. (WXT-2, Use of Relevant Historical Evidence)

Lesson 26: Social Darwinism vs.
the Social Gospel Movement

Multiple-Choice

1. The best answer is (C). The industrialists such as John D. Rockefeller/Andrew Carnegie embraced the ideas of William G. Sumner. He offered justification for their great financial empires and warned against government regulations that might reduce their profits and power. (WXT-2, Historical Causation)

2. The best answer is (A). The twentieth century economic debate was dominated by the question of how much government involvement the American economic system should tolerate. With the reforms the Progressive Era, the New Deal, and the Great Society, this question was at the forefront of all attempts to expand the government's economic power and to broaden social justice in the nation.
   (POL-3, Historical Causation, Continuity/Change)

Short-Answer

a. Answers will vary. With each of these acts the government expanded its reach and authority. They all extended help to different groups in society. They tended to challenge the American view of Social Darwinism and self-help that dominated much of the thinking of the Gilded Age. The Keating Owen Act was a federal law regulating child labor. The Hepburn Act regulated and restricted railroad activities and enlarged the Interstate Commerce Commission. Finally, the Pure Food and Drug Act regulated food and drug as it targeted prepared food and patent medicines. (POL-3, Use of Relevant Historical Evidence)

b. Answers will vary. The most likely examples of efforts to help the Forgotten Man would be the New Deal of the 1930s and the Great Society of the 1960s. Both followed in the traditions of the Social Gospel movement and the Progressive movement in attempting to change American society through government actions and programs. (POL-3, Use of Relevant Historical Evidence)

Lesson 27: Black Leaders, 1880–1968

Multiple-Choice

1. The best answer is (B). David Walker, a free black man in Boston, called for direct resistance to slavery and racism in the late 1820s. His manifesto was extremely radical for the times and its call for physical confrontations with the white power structure anticipated Malcolm X's message of attacking racism by any means necessary in the 1950s and the 1960s. (CUL-4, Use of Relevant Historical Evidence)

2. The best answer is (D). Malcolm X's call for segregation from whites, arming oneself for defense, and fighting back against discrimination was embraced by the Student Nonviolent Coordinating Committee as they developed their Black Power philosophy in the late 1960s. (CUL-4, Historical Causation)

Short-Answer

a. Answers will vary. Malcolm X preached an active, aggressive form of protest against racial discrimination. He wanted blacks to demand their rights and not tolerate discrimination or violence against themselves or their property. He agreed that racial equality was the ultimate goal of the civil rights movement, but he sought to achieve it by direct and possibly violent confrontation with the white establishment.
(CUL-4, Use of Relevant Historical Evidence)

b. Answers will vary. Several developments helped shape Malcolm X's view of the civil rights movement such as:

(1) his membership in the Nation of Islam;

(2) their militant views on segregation;

(3) the nation's growing interest in racial equality after World War II;

(4) Martin Luther King's non-violent approach to civil rights seemed too slow;

(5) there was a strong white back lash against expanding civil rights in the 1950s and 1960s;

(6) urban riots manifested a more militant approach to civil rights.

(CUL-4, Use of Relevant Historical Evidence)

c. Answers will vary. Malcolm X called on blacks to:

(1) support anti-colonialism in Africa;

(2) adopt Pan-African ideas;

(3) embrace the Muslim religion;

(4) be wary of mainstream civil rights ideas expressed by Martin Luther King;

(5) be willing to work with like minded whites (at the end of his life).

(NAT-4, Historical Causation)

Lesson 28: The Supreme Court and Government Regulation, 1890–1937

Multiple-Choice

1. The best answer is D. The Court drew a distinction between men and women regarding limitation on their working hours. In Lochner, a law that restricted men to working only ten hours was struck down. In Muller, however, the Court upheld a ten hour working limitation law for women because of their unique physical characteristics and their status as potential mothers. (NAT-2, Use of Relevant Historical Evidence)

2. The best answer is (A). In the mid-1930s the Supreme Court declared nine acts of the New Deal unconstitutional because it viewed various actions of government intervention in the private sector as excessive. The two most notable examples of these decisions were those that invalidated the Agricultural Adjustment Act and the National Industrial Recovery Act. (POL-3, Continuity/Change)

Short-Answer

a. Answers will vary. The National Women's Party would support Muller because it extended working protection to women. This could be a step in the direction of voting rights for women. The Bull Moose Party would not support Lochner because it restricted government power to regulate working hours and conditions. The Industrial Workers of the World would be opposed to both rulings because they did not go far enough to change the capitalist system. (NAT-1, Use of Relevant Historical Evidence)

b. Answers will vary. The Korematsu case upheld the right of the government to imprison Japanese Americans during World War II. It demonstrated that racial prejudice was very strong in the war years among many Americans. The Brown decision declared separate but equal schools unconstitutional. This demonstrated a slow recognition that the Jim Crow system must be disbanded. The Roe decision legalized abolition. The ruling gave women more control over their reproductive rights and helped fuel the feminist movement in the 1970s and 1980s. (NAT-2, Use of Relevant Historical Evidence)

Lesson 29: Reform Movements of the Twentieth Century

Multiple-Choice

1. The best answer is (C). In an approach similar to President Johnson's call to "broaden the base of abundance," the progressive reformers of the early 20th century hoped to improve the quality of life for women by regulating their working hours and conditions in American factories and businesses. (POL-3, Continuity/ Change)

2. The best answer is (A). Much of the conservative agenda of the 1980s was directed at scaling back the programs of the Great Society of the 1960s. The consensus among many people was that the federal government's size and spending policies had gotten out of hand. (POL-3, Continuity/Change, Historical Causation)

Short-Answer

a. Answers will vary. Each of these reform movements sought to extend the reach of the federal government into the lives of the poor, minorities, and, in the 1960s, women. Students should reference the 3 Rs of the New Deal, and the Great Society mission to complete Roosevelt's and Truman's reform agendas. (POL-3, Use of Relevant Historical Evidence)

b. In both eras there was intellectual support for action (the muckrakers in the Progressive Era and Michael Harrington's The Other America in the 1960s). There were strong Presidents in both eras (Theodore Roosevelt, Woodrow Wilson, and Lyndon Johnson). There was a belief that the gap between rich and poor was deleterious to the nation both philosophically and practically. The federal government had the financial and political resources to address some of the problems. (POL-3, Comparison)

c. Under the leadership of Lyndon Johnson, Congress enacted the Civil Rights Acts of 1964 and 1965, Head Start, the Job Corp, Food Stamps, Medicare, Medicaid, the Immigration Act of 1965, and over 70 bills for federal support for education. (POL-3, Use of Relevant Historical Evidence)

Lesson 30: Isolationism vs. Internationalism, 1919–1941

Multiple-Choice

1. The best answer is (C). George Washington's warning about entangling alliances dominated much of the foreign policy debate over America's role in European affairs in the nineteenth century. The issue of political/diplomatic isolationism carried over into the 1930s debate over America's role in Europe as war clouds began to gather there. (WOR-2, Continuity/Change, Contextualization)

2. The best answer is (D). When the North Atlantic Treaty Organization was proposed, many isolationists saw the alliance as a repudiation of the warning that George Washington gave in the late 1790s. The debate over joining the organization renewed the cry of avoiding "entangling foreign alliances." In fact, N.A.T.O. was the first time that the United States actually joined a formal European alliance. (WOR-2, Historical Causation)

Short-Answer

a. Answers will vary. The rejection of the Treaty of Versailles strengthened America's commitment to avoid European affairs. The nation rejected Article X's and collective security and curtailed American involvement in Europe for almost two decades. The Neutrality Acts prevented the United States from loaning money, providing weapons to belligerent nations, and prohibited American citizens from traveling into the war zone. These laws were the apex of isolationist sentiment in the 1930s. The Atlantic Charter pulled the United States closer to breaking its isolationism as America and Great Britain laid out a series of internationalist goals to be achieved when the fascists were defeated in Europe. (WOR-2, Historical Causation)

b. Answers will vary. Students might explain one of the following:

   (1) Washington's Neutrality Proclamation of 1793;

   (2) the Farewell Address of 1796;

   (3) overall neutrality in the Anglo-French conflict 1793-1812;

   (4) Monroe's restatement of Washington's policies in the Monroe Doctrine 1823.

   (WOR-2, Use of Relevant Historical Evidence)

c. Answers will vary. Students might explain the onset of the Cold War in the mid- and late 1940s, the Korean War, the Fall of China, and/or Soviet aggression in Greece, Iran and Eastern Europe. (WOR-2, Historical Causation, Contextulization)

Lesson 31: Transformation of Capitalism in the 1930s

Multiple-Choice

1. The best answer is (A). In the cartoon, the United States system of democracy and capitalism is symbolized by an old-fashion horse and buggy. Franklin Roosevelt is seen as offering a modern, state-of-the-art program of federal control. This debate over the degree of federal involvement in the lives of Americans continued throughout the nation's history. (POL-3, Continuity/Change, Historical Causation)

2. The best answer is (D). The question of federal control over the economy was raised when progressive reformers tried to curtail business and trust abuses in the early 20th century. Their use of the Sherman Act and Clayton Act raised controversy as did the New Deal programs of the 1930s. (POL-3, Continuity/Change, Contextualization)

Short-Answer

a. Answers will vary. Harry Hopkins, a principal strategist for the New Deal, would support the idea of federal government control in the economy. Norman Thomas, a socialist, would want much more federal control of the economy and social system than the New Deal offered. Herbert Hoover, a Republican, would caution against too much federal control. He would fear that such actions would lead to totalitarianism. (POL-3, Use of Relevant Historical Evidence)

b. Answers will vary. (POL-3, Historical Causation)

c. Answers will vary. Students might explain various elements of the 3 Rs such as the National Industrial Recovery Act, Agricultural Adjustment Act, Glass-Steagall Act, Social Security Act, Wagner Act, Federal Emergency Relief Act, Tennessee Valley Authority Act, Civil Works Administration, Works Progress Administration. (POL-3, Use of Relevant Historical Evidence)

Lesson 32: Presidential Civil Rights Records, 1945–1974

Multiple-Choice

1. The best answer is (B). The Little Rock crisis flowed from the *Brown v. Board of Education* decision of 1954. This ruling overturned the separate but equal doctrine that had been in place since 1896. Attempts to integrate the schools of Little Rock resulted in mob violence and intimidation. This resistance prompted President Eisenhower to send troops to quell the disorders. (NAT-2, Historical Causation)

2. The best answer is (C). During the Reconstruction era, federal troops were dispatched to force the South to abide by the Radical Reconstruction program, and to put down the

violence of the Ku Klux Klan. By 1876 most of the 20,000 troops that had occupied the South had been withdrawn and Reconstruction was over. (POL-3, Contextualization, Comparison)

Short-Answer

a. Answers will vary. The Brown decision was the catalyst for the desegregation of the schools when the court struck down the separate but equal doctrine. This was the cause of the violence in Little Rock. The Southern Manifesto was a statement signed by 101 southern Congressmen denouncing the Brown decision as "a clear abuse of judicial power." *To Secure These Rights* was a report to President Truman that placed the executive branch behind an expansion of civil rights. It helped awaken the country to the plight of African Americans and set a precedent for future President to be more involved in the equal rights movement. (POL-1, Historical Causation)

b. Answers will vary. Students might explain *To Secure These Rights* as the best example since it was the first real attempt by a modern President (Truman) to put civil rights on the national political agenda in a meaningful way. Others might cite the Brown decision since it overturned *Plessy v. Ferguson*, which was the bedrock of Jim Crow system. (POL-1, Periodization)

c. Students should recognize and explain that the "Southern Manifesto" was not in tune with the onset of the modern civil rights era. In fact, it was a pledge by southern members of Congress to block any changes in the Jim Crow system. (POL-1, Periodization, Use of Relevant Historical Evidence)

Lesson 33: Containment, 1945–1975

Multiple-Choice

1. The best answer is (D). As a result of the economic collapse in most of Western Europe after the war, the United States believed it must reject its pre-war isolationism and become more engaged in European affairs. (WOR-2, Historical Causation, Contextualization)

2. The best answer is (A). The United States began a series of economic and financial programs after the war to stabilize European economies and to keep the countries from turning to alternative political and economic systems such as communism. (WOR-2, Historical Causation)

Short-Answer

a. Answers will vary. The Truman Doctrine was the first aid program established in 1947. It provided $400 million in economic assistance to Greece and Turkey. The Marshall Plan was grander is scope as it involved $22 billion of aid to most of Western Europe from 1947-1952. The North Atlantic Treaty Organization was the first time the United States joined a military alliance. It was designed to safeguard Western Europe from a military attack by the Soviet Union. (WOR-2, Historical Causation)

b. Answers will vary. The United States rejected its isolationist policies of the past and became deeply involved in collective security arrangements in Europe and elsewhere in the world. The nation came to see the communist threat as worldwide. (WOR-2, Periodization)

c. After the fall of Vietnam in 1975 to the communists, the United States became less interested in assisting other nations either militarily or economically. We turned inward to address domestic problems that affected the nation. (WOR-2, Contextualization, Use of Relevant Historical Evidence)

Lesson 34: Failure of Containment— The Vietnam War

Multiple-Choice

1. The best answer is (D). While there was a significant anti-war movement in the United States by 1967, many Americans questioned whether it was patriotic to protest an overseas war while American soldiers were in danger on the battlefield. This question was debated throughout American history from the Hartford Convention during the War of 1812 to the anti-war marches on Washington in the 1960s and 1970s.
(POL-2, NAT-3, Continuity/Change)

2. The best answer is (C). The protest movement raised debate about the justification for the war in Vietnam in both the Republican and Democratic parties. The greatest turmoil, however, was among Democrats. The conflict was so great that President Johnson decided not to seek another term as president in 1968. (POL-2, NAT-3, Historical Causation)

Short-Answer

a. Answers will vary. The Student Nonviolent Coordinating Committee, while ostensibly concerned with civil rights, supported the protest over the war. Its members believed young black men bore a disproportional burden of the fighting. The Students for a Democratic Society supported the idea of stopping the war. They were likely participants in the protest depicted in the photograph. A World War II veteran would likely believe the protest were wrongheaded and unpatriotic. He would believe that all Americans should rally round the flag. (POL-2, Use of Relevant Historical Evidence)

b. Answers will vary. (POL-2, Use of Relevant Historical Evidence)

c. Answers will vary. Students might explain one of the following protests during war time:

(1) Loyalists during the American Revolution;

(2) the Hartford Convention during the War of 1812;

(3) the Abolitionists and Transcendentalists during the Mexican War;

(4) Copperheads during the Civil War;

(5) the Anti-Imperialist League members during the Spanish American War;

(6) Socialist who protested during World War I (Eugene Debs).

(POL-2, Use of Relevant Historical Evidence)

Lesson 35: Famous Doctrines— from Monroe to Nixon

Multiple-Choice

1. The best answer is (A). The Monroe Doctrine became the foundation for America's aggressive foreign policy in the late 19th century and early 20th century. President Theodore Roosevelt, in particular, expanded the original Doctrine to include a broader justification for American intervention in Latin American affairs.
   (WOR-2, Continuity/Change, Historical Causation)

2. The best answer is (B). The non-involvement in European affairs of the Monroe Doctrine was a reinforcement of the isolationist policy set forth by George Washington during his administration. (NAT-3, Historical Causation)

Short-Answer

a. President Monroe set forth the following principles:

   (1) no further colonization in Latin America by European powers;

   (2) no establishment of new monarchies in Latin America;

   (3) non interference with existing Latin American colonies or with European affairs.

   (WOR-2, Use of Relevant Historical Evidence)

b. The Big Stick Policy grew directly from the Monroe Doctrine. Its aggressive approach to managing the events in Latin America was an extension of the 1823 warning. Dollar Diplomacy was a variation on the Big Stick Policy. If a country failed to respond to financial assistance (or pressure) then the United States would resort to the Big Stick. The Good Neighbor Policy of the late 1920s and 1930s attempted to soften the intervention edge of the Monroe Doctrine by trying to cooperate with Latin America through multi-lateral agreements and actions. (WOR-2, Historical Causation)

c. Answers will vary. The United States changed its stance toward Latin America in the 1820s because:

   (1) Many Latin American countries had become independent from 1810-1823;

   (2) There were rumors that the Holy Alliance was forming to help Spain recover her colonies;

(3) The United States was in the midst of a nationalistic period that the Monroe Doctrine reflected. The reason for the continuity in the Doctrine was its restatement of America's policy of the long-time tradition of non-involvement in European affairs dating back to the earliest days of the Republic. (WOR-2, Continuity/ Change)

Long Essay Questions

with Suggested Responses

The 17 Long Essay Questions that follow are available on the Teacher Companion Website so that you can easily print and copy for your students, or copy/paste into your own assessment activities. Please note that the suggested responses begin on page 57.

Question 1

Evaluate the extent to which political and religious dissent shaped colonial development in New England and the Chesapeake regions from 1619–1750.

(NAT-1, POL-1; Change over Time and Causation; Lessons 1, 2)

Question 2

"America's greatest presidents transformed and strengthened the relationship between the government and the people."

Evaluate this statement by comparing and contrasting the policies of TWO United States presidents with regards to their views on the role of government in society.

(POL-1, POL-3; Comparison and Contrast; Lessons 3, 16, 29, 31)

Question 3

Historians often consider Thomas Jefferson a liberal and Alexander Hamilton a conservative leader in the 1790s. To what extent is this assessment valid about the two men's political philosophy and actions in the era?

(POL-1; Comparison; Lessons 7, 8, 10)

Question 4

Evaluate the extent to which political compromises maintained continuity as well as promoted change in American politics from 1787–1850.

(POL-1; Continuity and Change; Lesson 13)

Question 5

Evaluate the extent to which the struggle between liberals and conservatives from 1940 to 1980 was part of the presidential legacy of Franklin Roosevelt.

(POL-3; Change over Time and Causation; Lessons 8, 9, 29, 31)

Question 6

Evaluate the extent to which the platforms and beliefs of political parties promoted the coming of the Civil War from 1840–1860.

(POL-1; Change over Time and Causation; Lessons 10, 11)

Question 7

Evaluate the extent to which the Federalist Party contributed to the development of the American economic system from 1790–1825.

(POL-3; Change over Time and Causation; Lessons 7, 10, 14)

Question 8

Evaluate the extent to which the ideas of the Second Great Awakening and the development of utopian societies in the 1830s and 1840s maintained continuity as well as promoted changes in Americans' views of themselves and their society.

(POL-2; Continuity and Change; Lessons 5, 19)

Question 9

To what extent did nineteenth century armed conflicts represent a turning point and a new direction in American foreign policy?

(WOR-2; Periodization; Lessons 12, 16, 17)

Question 10

Compare and contrast the successes and failures of the abolitionist and women's movements in expanding democracy in the nineteenth century.

(POL-2; Comparison and Contrast; Lessons 11, 20, 21)

Question 11

Evaluate the extent to which Congress and the Supreme Court helped the South win the peace after the Civil War.

Consider the years 1868–1900.

(POL-3, NAT-2; Causation; Lessons 23, 24)

Question 12

Analyze the main issues that framed the debate over the appropriate role of the federal government in the American economy from 1880–1910.

(POL-3; Change over Time; Lessons 25, 26, 28)

Question 13

Compare and contrast the role of TWO civil rights leaders in combating the Jim Crow system from 1890–1925.

(POL-2; Comparison and Contrast; Lesson 27)

Question 14

Evaluate the extent to which political and economic reform movements promoted social justice in the United States from 1900–1940

Consider at least TWO movements.

(POL-2; Change over Time and Causation; Lesson 9, 29, 31)

Question 15

Evaluate the extent to which American foreign policy from 1920–1941 maintained continuity as well as promoted change in America's view of itself in world affairs.

(WOR-2; Continuity and Change; Lessons 22, 30)

Question 16

Some historians have suggested that private individuals rather than political figures played a greater role in promoting civil rights after World War II.

Support, modify, or refute this interpretation providing specific evidence from the contributions of at least two individuals from 1945–1969 to justify your answer.

(POL-2; Causation; Lesson 27, 32)

Question 17

Compare and contrast the successes and failures of containment of TWO Cold War presidents from 1945–1974.

(WOR-2; Compare and Contrast; Lessons 33, 34, 35)

Long Essay Question 1

Evaluate the extent to which political and religious dissent shaped colonial development in New England and the Chesapeake regions from 1619-1750.

(NAT-1, POL-1; Change over Time and Causation; Lessons 1, 2)

Students can use a variety facts and ideas to answer this prompt. In addition to the information in Lessons 1 and 2, your students could include some of the following ideas:

OVERALL THEMES

1. In New England the intolerance and inflexible religious attitudes of the Puritans, especially in the early years, caused clashes and encouraged splinter religious groups to form.

2. In the Chesapeake region, Bacon's Rebellion had a direct impact on the labor system. Virginia became increasingly alarmed about the indentured servant system after the revolt, and began to rely more heavily on slavery.

3. The Great Awakening of the 1730s and 1740s reflected an attempt to promote Calvinist religious views, challenge established church authority, and increase religious freedom.

POSSIBLE INFORMATION

Puritan Religious Beliefs

- wanted to create a "city upon a hill"
- believed they had "the true religion and holy ordinance of Almighty God"
- believed "if God be with us, who can be against us"
- only one true way to God
- people better whipped than damned
- strong enforcement of religious procedures

Roger Williams

- called for separation of Church and State
- fairer treatment of Native Americans
- public denunciation of the Church of England
- opposed requiring non-church members to go to church
- banished from Massachusetts Bay in 1635
- founder of Rhode Island with very liberal religious views

Anne Hutchinson

- challenged Puritans in Massachusetts Bay
- spoke out against idea that salvation could be achieved through good works
- wanted to discuss and interpret sermons
- publicly criticized ministers
- claimed God had spoken directly to her
- "troubled the peace of the commonwealth"
- did not know "her place" as a woman
- acted more like "husband than a wife"
- banished in 1638
- traveled from place to place after banishment
- killed by Indians in 1643

Thomas Hooker

- believed Massachusetts Bay was too narrow in its teachings
- said godly people could be admitted to church membership even if they had not had conversion experience
- people should be able to elect officials and then guide their decisions
- left Massachusetts in 1635
- settled in Hartford, Connecticut
- 1639 helped to write Fundamental Orders of Connecticut
- Orders allowed all freemen, whether church members or not, to vote

Mary Dyer and the Quakers

- Puritans made it clear Quakers were not welcome in colony
- Quakers believed in many roads to God
- all people had light of God within them
- Quakers seen as dangerous, seditious by Puritans
- during mid-1650s Puritans punished Quakers who tried to practice religion
- 1658 passed law that prescribed death to Quakers for worshipping in Massachusetts
- 1660 executed Mary Dyer for her religious activities
- this persecution began to undermine the Crown's confidence that Massachusetts should keep its charter; lost it in 1690s

Great Awakening

- a religious revival in 1730s and 1740s
- led by George Whitefield and Jonathan Edwards
- an attempt to combat the growing secularism of the colonies
- Calvinist in its message
- return to Calvinist views of:
  - predestination
  - original sin

- a harsh and angry God
- message summarized by Edwards' "Sinners in the Hands of an Angry God"
- promoted religious pluralism

Political Dissent: Bacon's Rebellion

- 1676
- caused by frontier clashes with Native Americans
- Bacon and his followers wanted to attack Native Americans to gain their land
- Governor William Berkeley said no
- Bacon and his men marched against Jamestown
- briefly ousted Berkeley
- rebellion collapsed when Bacon died
- Bacon's forces included many black/white former indentured servants
- rebellion had several levels of significance:
  - made Virginia question the indentured servant system
  - colony turned increasingly to permanent African slavery to solve labor problems
  - some historians view it as first attack on insensitive, autocratic British rule, as a prelude to the American Revolution

Long Essay Question 2

"America's greatest presidents transformed and strengthened the relationship between the government and the people."

Evaluate this statement by comparing and contrasting the policies of TWO United States presidents with regards to their views on the role of government in society.

(POL-1, POL-3; Comparison and Contrast; Lessons 3, 16, 29, 31)

Students could select among several presidents to answer this prompt. In addition to the information in Lessons 3, 16, 29, 31, your students might select the three presidents most likely to be rated as great: Thomas Jefferson, Abraham Lincoln, and Franklin Roosevelt. Your students could also include some of the following:

OVERALL THEMES

1. Each of these men enhanced the powers of the presidency to assist the people. In all cases, they expanded the executive power in government at the expense of the Congress through bold action and superb political skills.

2. All three men were excellent politicians, that is, manipulators of men and controllers of Congress. Also, they were able to communicate their vision of America's future to the people.

3. All reversed the direction of the country when they took power. They altered the policies of their discredited predecessor in the White House.

4. All were strong partisans who transformed their parties into dominant political forces for years to come.

5. Each man viewed the role of government in a different way. Jefferson sought to limit the role of government, while both Abraham Lincoln and Franklin Roosevelt, for different reasons, expanded it.

POSSIBLE INFORMATION

Thomas Jefferson

- reversed the elitist, centralizing political attitudes of the Federalists, especially John Adams' last two years in power (Sedition Act, Alien Acts, and "midnight judges")
- presided over the first transfer of power between the two political factions
- set the nation on a path of decentralization that marked America as unique in the era of monarchies
- his policies:
  - created a government favorable to independent yeoman farmers
  - reduced the concentration of power in the central government
  - abolished excise taxes on such items as whiskey
  - pardoned the victims of the Sedition Act
  - repealed the Judiciary Act of 1801
  - doubled the size of the United States through the Louisiana Purchase 1803
  - cut national debt from $83 million to $45 million
- his election in 1800 placed the government on a frugal, more egalitarian path
- began the "Virginia Dynasty" (1801–1825) of Democratic-Republican presidents, all from Virginia
- followed by James Madison and James Monroe

Abraham Lincoln

- reversed James Buchanan's weak response to secession
- restored the Union—his greatest achievement
- ended slavery—slowly and reluctantly—but he did it
- by saving the Union and ending slavery he reaffirmed and strengthened the ideals of the Declaration of Independence and Constitution
- kept foreign nations out of the Civil War and isolated the South diplomatically
- persuaded Congress to:
  - pass the Homestead Act of 1862, which opened the west to settlement by giving away land
  - begin to build the transcontinental railroad (completed 1869)
  - create a national banking system with the National Banking Acts of 1863–1864
- was the first of four consecutive Republican presidents elected from 1860–1880

Franklin Roosevelt

- energized the country and restored hope after economy reached its nadir during the last year of the Hoover presidency
- expanded the federal government's efforts to combat the Great Depression
- communicated to the people that the government had not forgotten them
- doubled the amount of money spent by Hoover
- administered direct relief to the people who could not work
- expanded the federal government's role in the health, education, and welfare of the American people
- extended government regulation of the banking industry and stock market
- created the Social Security system to help the elderly
- restored the nation's faith in democracy and capitalism and increased its expectation for government action in economic hard times
- alleviated the suffering of millions of Americans
- led the nation through World War II
- established the Democrats as the dominant political party for the next 35 years

Long Essay Question 3

Historians often consider Thomas Jefferson a liberal and Alexander Hamilton a conservative leader in the 1790s. To what extent is this assessment valid about the two men's political philosophy and actions in the era?

(POL-1; Comparison; Lessons 7, 8, 10)

Students can use many facts and ideas to answer this prompt. In addition to the information in Lessons 7, 8, and 10, your students could include some of the following ideas:

OVERALL THEMES

1. Hamilton represented the conservative position of the 1790s. He believed that America would thrive under a strong central government with a concentration of financial and military power at the national level.

2. Since monarchies ruled Europe at this time, Hamilton's philosophy represented the status quo (conservative) thinking of the 1790s.

3. Throughout Europe during the 1790s, strong central governments ruled with little or no input from the governed.

4. Jefferson's ideas represented a challenge to this thinking, thus he was a liberal.

5. Jefferson sought a political system that promoted decentralization of power, states' rights, and an active, vocal role for the "people" (i.e., yeoman farmers).

POSSIBLE INFORMATION

Hamilton's Conservative Position:

- national government must have power
- national government and mercantile interests must cooperate for economic progress
- Congress and the president should expand their authority through the "necessary and proper clause" (elastic clause)
- nation would benefit from the creation/existence of a National Bank
- national debt should be funded at par value, but not paid off too quickly
- tariffs and other taxes must remain high to pay down the debt
- the "common people" should allow the elites to govern the nation
- opposition such as the Whiskey Rebellion should be repressed decisively and forcefully
- good commercial and political relations with Great Britain should be the sine qua non of America's foreign policy

Jefferson's Liberal Position:

- states should maintain as much power as possible
- agrarian interests should be promoted and protected by the government
- the Constitution must be strictly interpreted; the elastic clause should not be stretched
- the national debt is harmful and should be eliminated as quickly as possible
- taxes such as the one on whiskey are oppressive and impose too much control by the central government over people's lives
- government should heed the people's protests
- government should encourage average people to participate in its decision-making
- America should align itself with the antimonarchical philosophy sweeping France during the French Revolution

Long Essay Question 4

Evaluate the extent to which political compromises maintained continuity as well as promoted change in American politics from 1787–1850.

(POL-1; Continuity and Change; Lesson 13)

Students can use a variety of facts and ideas to answer this prompt. In addition to the information in Lesson 12, your students could include some of the following ideas:

OVERALL THEMES

1. The question of representation in Congress dominated the Constitutional Convention. The delegates expected Congress to be the most important branch of government. With state sovereignty in the forefront of the delegates' minds, representation in Congress was the number-one issue to be resolved.

2. As slavery became more important economically in the South, its preservation and extension became a growing controversy between the two sections.

3. On two occasions in the 1820s and 1850s, the nation reached an impasse over the extension of slavery into the territories.

4. Both compromises postponed a national crisis over the issue of slavery.

POSSIBLE INFORMATION

The Great Compromise

- sometimes called the Connecticut Compromise
- reached July 12, 1787
- a blend of the Virginia and New Jersey Plans
- both plans called for strengthening the powers of Congress
- Virginia Plan based congressional representation on population:
  - two houses of Congress
  - lower house determined by state population
  - upper house elected by lower house
- New Jersey Plan called for one house of Congress with each state having one vote gave Congress more taxing power and regulatory authority retained unicameral aspect of legislature as it had existed under Articles of Confederation
- Compromise:
  - two houses of Congress
  - lower house based on population
  - upper house with equal representation from each state
  - all money bills start in lower house (House of Representatives)
- Compromise broke deadlock between small and large states and allowed the convention to continue its work in creating the Constitution

The Missouri Compromise

- also called Compromise of 1820
- Missouri applied for statehood in 1819 as slave state
- there was a balance of 11 free and 11 slave states
- since the Articles of Confederation, states had entered union in pairs—one free, one slave
- South believed Missouri, as part of Louisiana Territory, should maintain its status as slave territory
- February 1819, James Tallmadge from New York introduced a resolution that slavery be gradually ended in Missouri after it became a state
- his proposal roiled Congress
- Speaker of the House Henry Clay proposed a compromise:
  - Missouri would become a slave state;
  - Maine would become a free state;
  - a line dividing the Louisiana Territory into a northern free area; and

- a southern slave area would be established (at 36° and 30' North latitude)
- while the South opposed dividing the Louisiana Territory, the Compromise narrowly passed
- Clay's Compromise partially restored sectional harmony; the agreement held until 1854 when the Kansas-Nebraska Act opened territory north of the 36° 30' line to slavery

Compromise of 1850

- December 1849, California sought admission to Union as a free state
- South opposed the move because it would disrupt balance in Senate (15 free and 15 slave)
- an aging Henry Clay tried one last compromise:
  - California enters as a free state
  - formation of territorial government in Mexican Cession with status of slavery to be determined by popular sovereignty
  - abolition of slave trade in District of Columbia, but retention of slavery there
  - stronger Fugitive Slave Law
- Clay failed to get the package passed, and he withdrew
- Stephen Douglas stepped forward and, after the death of John C. Calhoun and President Zachary Taylor (both of whom opposed the measure), shepherded the compromise through Congress
- provided only short-term solutions to a growing problem over slavery in territories
- much less effective than Missouri Compromise
- did suppress movement for secession among southerners at the Nashville Convention in 1850
- delayed Civil War for 11 years, giving North time to expand advantage over South in population and industrialization

Long Essay Question 5

Evaluate the extent to which the struggle between liberals and conservatives from 1940 to 1980 was part of the presidential legacy of Franklin Roosevelt.

(POL-3; Change over Time and Causation; Lessons 8, 9, 29, 31)

Students can use many facts and ideas to answer this prompt. In addition to the information in Lessons 8, 9, 29, and 31, your students could include some of the following ideas:

OVERALL THEMES

1. From 1940–1980 the major division between liberal and conservatives was the question of the role of the federal government in domestic affairs. The New Deal was the catalyst for this debate, with its unprecedented expansion of government power in the 1930s.

2. For liberals who supported government activism, the expansion of the New Deal was a measure of America's commitment to the "forgotten man" (average people) of America.

3. For conservatives, who questioned the consequences of government activism on American political and economic institutions, the issue was which parts of the New Deal to accept, which programs to limit, and which programs to eliminate.

4. Although the New Deal had no civil rights program in the 1930s, after 1954 the issue of minority rights also divided conservatives and liberals, with conservatives resisting government intervention on behalf of minorities and liberals promoting government assistance in achieving equality.

POSSIBLE INFORMATION

Harry Truman
- his Fair Deal was clearly an attempt to continue the New Deal agenda
- he increased the minimum wage
- he signed the National Housing Act, providing 800,000 low-cost housing units
- he expanded Social Security benefits
- he signed G.I. Bill of Rights
- he signed Full Employment Act, committing government to managing economy
- he proposed:
  ○ national health insurance
  ○ a civil rights program that included a national antilynching law
- he signed Executive Order 9981, which desegregated the military

Dwight Eisenhower
- called his program "Modern Republicanism"
- hoped to reverse the direction of New Deal, but accepted much of it
- called for a "pay as you go" approach to social spending—balance the budget
- he removed wage and price controls
- lowered price supports for farm products
- kept Social Security (actually expanded it)
- increased minimum wage
- created Department of Health, Education, and Welfare
- Highway Act (1956) $31 billion for interstate highway system
- National Defense Education Act (1958)
- little support for civil rights

John Kennedy
- proposed expansion of the New Deal, but little actually accomplished
- proposed:
  ○ national health insurance (Medicare)
  ○ extension of unemployment benefits
  ○ Civil Rights Act (1963)

- accomplished:
  - increase of minimum wage
  - broadening of Social Security
  - Area Redevelopment Act—federal aid for poor regions
  - Manpower Development and Training Act—$435 million to train workers
  - establishment of a Women's Bureau in Labor Department and enactment of Equal Pay Act
- more style than substance domestically yet dedicated to an active role for government

Lyndon Johnson

- the president most committed to completing the New Deal
- he had most ambitious and successful domestic program of the twentieth century
- with his "War on Poverty" he changed the face of the welfare state
- he accomplished:
  - a tax cut
  - Food Stamp program
  - Civil Rights Act of 1964 and Voting Rights Act of 1965
  - Medicare and Medicaid
  - Economic Opportunity Act (Head Start, Job Corps)
  - Office of Economic Opportunity
  - more than sixty education bills
- percentage of Americans in poverty fell from 20 percent in 1963 to 13 percent in 1968
- his administration represented the high point of twentieth-century liberalism

Richard Nixon

- a moderate Republican in the mold of Eisenhower
- accomplished:
  - increased federal funding for low-cost housing
  - increased spending on mandated social programs
  - Environmental Protection Act
  - Occupational Safety and Health Administration
  - Consumer Product Safety Act
  - Clean Water Act
  - National Air Quality Standards Act
- proposed:
  - a major overhaul of welfare system—Family Assistance Plan
- accepted that big government was here to stay
- on civil rights:
  - first two years showed moderate support for civil rights by expanding
  - minority hiring and contracting programs

◦ by 1971, had turned against civil rights by opposing busing, attempting to put conservatives on Supreme Court

Jimmy Carter

- inflation and economic stagnation undermined Carter's support for the New Deal ideals

- a growing generational split emerged during the Carter years as younger Democrats began to wonder whether massive government programs were impeding economic development

- many Democrats opposed higher taxes and expanded social programs

- Carter: "more [government] is not necessarily better"

- maintained rather than expanded the core of the New Deal/Fair Deal/Great Society

- he tended to admire Fair Deal Democrats more than the New Dealers

Long Essay Question 6

Evaluate the extent to which the platforms and beliefs of political parties promoted the coming of the Civil War from 1840–1860.

(POL-1; Change over Time and Causation; Lessons 10, 11)

Students can use a variety of facts and ideas to answer this prompt. In addition to the information in Lessons 10 and 11, your students could include some of the following ideas:

OVERALL THEMES

1. All three parties were caught in the dispute over slavery in the late 1840s and 1850s.

2. Each of the parties addressed the question of where slavery should be allowed to expand and whether it should be tolerated in the southern states.

3. All three parties were buffeted by the issue.

4. None of the parties called for the immediate abolition of slavery, but they all played a role in dividing the nation.

5. The Republican Party eventually became the political home for most members of the other two parties.

POSSIBLE INFORMATION

Liberty/Free Soil Party

- Liberty Party formed in 1840; in 1848 it was "translated" into the Free Soil Party

- 1840, 1844 Liberty Party ran James Birney for president

- 1844 Birney drew votes from Clay, giving victory to Polk

- 1848 Free Soil Party nominated Martin Van Buren and 1852 John P. Hale

- by 1854 Free Soil Party had been absorbed into the Republican Party
- platform:
  - abolish slavery wherever constitutionally possible
  - end slavery in Washington D.C.
  - 1844 opposed annexation of Texas
- endorsed:
  - cheap postage
  - internal improvements
  - limiting government spending
  - free homesteads
  - a tariff for revenue only
- motto: "free soil, free speech, free labor and free men"
- in 1852 Hale denounced the Compromise of 1850, called for the repeal of the Fugitive Slave Law
- impact: weakened the Whig Party, inserted slavery into the political arena, paved way for Republican Party of 1850s

The American Party

- nicknamed "Know Nothings"
- antiforeign and anti-Catholic
- very strong in early 1850s—many thought they could replace the Whigs as a second major party
- tried to link Catholics to slavery; claimed Catholics were trying to spread slavery
- hoped to avoid the divisive issue of slavery by focusing on immigrant threat
- many saw them as the party that might preserve the nation's purity and the Union
- captured control of several state legislatures, dozens of seats in Congress
- by 1855, the party had split over slavery
- platform:
  - extend naturalization period from five to twenty-one years
  - literacy test to vote
  - tax on immigrants
  - supported temperance laws
  - opposed Fugitive Slave Law
  - opposed Kansas-Nebraska Act
  - condemned "Rum, Romanism and Slavery"
  - anti-Catholic, especially opposed to separate parochial schools
- impact: by emphasizing an issue other than slavery, the party hoped to draw support, but it became enmeshed in the controversy just like other political groups

The Republican Party

- formed in response to the passage of the Kansas-Nebraska Act 1854

- clearly a sectional party (North and West)
- not abolitionists—made clear the party favored the interests of the white man
- dedicated to fighting "the slave power conspiracy" of the South
- platform:
  - motto: "free soil, free labor, and free men"
  - opposed the spread of slavery into the territories
  - no interference with slavery in the southern states
  - supported high protective tariff
  - favored government program of internal improvements—especially railroads
  - supported a homestead act
- impact: although not directly attacking slavery, the Republican Party was seen by the South as a threat to the institution and the southern way of life; its founding set stage for a major political confrontation
- 1860 election of Republican Abraham Lincoln led several southern states to secede from the Union

Long Essay Question 7

Evaluate the extent to which the Federalist Party contributed to the development of the American economic system from 1790–1825.

(POL-3; Change over Time and Causation; Lessons 7, 10, 14)

Students can use a variety of facts and ideas to answer this prompt. In addition to the information in Lessons 7, 10, and 14, your students could include some of the following ideas:

OVERALL THEMES

1. The Federalist Party's economic policy favored and supported the mercantile, commercial interests in the United States during the nation's formative period.

2. The Federalists established the financial foundation of the country with the creation of the National Bank and the tax system.

3. The Federalists sought to strengthen America's economic self-sufficiency by enhancing manufacturing and commerce.

4. The Federalists hoped to see the nation linked more closely by roads and canals that would expand markets and make raw materials more accessible to businesses.

POSSIBLE INFORMATION

Hamilton's Financial Plan

- creation of a National Bank

- assumption of states' debt
- payment of debt at par value
- excise tax on whiskey, other products
- Report on Manufactures (1791) called for tariff designed to raise revenue and to protect American manufacturing interests

Republicans' Adoption of Federalists' Ideas

- after War of 1812, Henry Clay proposed "American System," an updated version of the Federalist economic blueprint; it included:
  - a second national bank (established 1816)
  - a protective tariff (Tariff of 1816)
  - increased spending on internal improvements (roads and canals); however, Bonus Bill, providing federal funding for these, was vetoed by Madison

Marshall's Court and the Federalist Tradition

- John Marshall served as Chief Justice of Supreme Court, 1801–1835
- Led Court to uphold Federalist economic principles
- *McCulloch v. Maryland* 1819—decided National Bank was constitutional
- Dartmouth College Case 1819—strengthened sanctity of contracts, encouraging commerce
- *Gibbons v. Ogden* 1824—struck down monopolies, affirmed federal power over interstate commerce

Long Essay Question 8

Evaluate the extent to which the ideas of the Second Great Awakening and the development of utopian societies in the 1830s and 1840s maintained continuity as well as promoted changes in Americans' views of themselves and their society.

(POL-2; Continuity and Change; Lessons 5, 19)

Students can use a variety of facts and ideas to answer this prompt. In addition to the information in Lessons 5 and 19, your students could include some of the following ideas:

OVERALL THEMES

The changing nature of identity might include Americans:

1. continued belief in democracy and capitalism

2. continued belief in the righteousness of the people

3. continued belief in progress and improvement for society

4. supporting the expansion of democratic ideals

5. questioning (women and African Americans) their inferiority in the American political and social system

6. worrying about their personal salvation and the direction of society

7. replacing secular materialism with a commitment to helping others

8. taking greater responsibility for their lives and personal salvation

9. considering themselves "free moral agents"

POSSIBLE INFORMATION

The Second Great Awakening contributed to these changes with:

- belief in personal and societal perfection
- belief that salvation could be earned by good works
- belief in personal effort and free will
- rejection of the materialism of the Market Revolution
- accepting equality for all people before God
- praising human abilities and activities
- belief in universal salvation for those who sought it
- trying to establish a "Benevolent Empire" on earth

Utopian societies contributed to a changing identity by:

- replacing competitive individualism with a spiritual unity and group cooperation
- belief in perfectionism and millennialism
- accepting unusual sexual arrangement between members (in some cases)
- promoting great equality and authority for women
- attempting to abolish social divisions and injustices
- countering perceived social degradation that accompanied the Market Revolution
- rejecting capitalism and accepting a socialistic economic order
- trying to create a new moral world

Long Essay Question 9

To what extent did nineteenth-century armed conflicts represent a turning point and a new direction in American foreign policy?

Consider TWO conflicts in your answer.

(WOR-2; Periodization; Lessons 12, 16, 17)

Students can use a variety of facts and ideas to answer this prompt. In addition to the information in lessons 12, 16, and 17, your students could include some of the following ideas:

OVERALL THEMES

1. Attempts by the United States to settle disputes through warfare with other countries produced mixed results in the nineteenth century.

2. In all three conflicts the United States sought territory owned by other countries.

3. Only in the Mexican-American War did the United States achieve clear ownership and control over the coveted land (Mexican Cession and disputed parts of Texas).

4. The War of 1812 brought on new economic and political relationships with Great Britain and Europe.

5. The Mexican War, with the addition of the Mexican Cession, divided the nation further and made the Civil War more likely.

6. The Spanish-American War made the United States a world, colonial power.

POSSIBLE INFORMATION

War of 1812

- causes:
  - United States wanted to defend its honor on seas
  - hoped to maintain neutrality in war between England and France
  - United States wanted to stop British maritime interference
  - humiliated by impressments of American sailors
  - United States hoped to acquire land in Canada and Florida
  - United States angry that British were inciting Native Americans to attack in Ohio and Indiana
- results:
  - war ended with the restoration of the status quo ante
  - no territorial changes
  - British stopped seizure of ships and impressment, but not because of American military pressure
  - British agreed to abandon western forts and stop inciting Indians
  - war sparked a feeling of nationalism because we stood up against England
- political/diplomatic impact:
  - mixed diplomatic record for the United States
  - America did not gain land it wanted
  - showed America's willingness to defend honor and protect rights on the seas
  - yet United States went to war prematurely in 1812; problems could have been solved at bargaining table

Mexican-American War

- causes:
  - America annexed Texas in March 1845
  - Mexico claimed it owned Texas; did not recognize the Treaty of Velasco (1836)

- United States tried to negotiate, buy land, settle boundary at Rio Grande
- President Polk sent John Slidell to settle issues, but reached no diplomatic agreement
- border clash between the United States and Mexico in April 1846; in May, Polk asked for declaration of war

- results:
  - Treaty of Guadalupe Hidalgo signed February 2, 1848
    - » Mexico recognized Texas independence, surrendered the Mexican Cession, and agreed to Rio Grande as Texas border
    - » United States paid Mexico $15 million for land (529,000 square miles, 48 cents per acre)
    - » Mexican Cession included California, New Mexico, Utah, and many other western states
    - » America assumed financial claims its new citizens still had against Mexico

- political/diplomatic impact:
  - Mexican Cession became a "dose of poison" for the United States because it raised divisive slavery issue
  - Wilmot Proviso, calling for ban on slavery in newly acquired territories, led to increasingly bitter arguments
  - set off sectional dispute that helped divide nation and brought on Civil War
  - soured relations with Mexico for decades to come

Spanish-American War

- causes:
  - uprising among Cubans against Spanish rule in 1895 was principal cause
  - United States businesses had $50 million invested in Cuban sugar industry
  - U.S. had $100 million in trade with Cuba
  - part of a general imperialistic mood of the 1890s

- other causes:
  - yellow press—William Randolph Hearst's and Joseph Pulitzer's sensational news stories about Spanish atrocities
  - DeLôme letter criticizing McKinley
  - destruction of battleship Maine
  - United States gave Spain an ultimatum:
    - » immediate armistice with rebels
    - » stop brutal treatment and killing of Cubans
    - » release prisoners
    - » allow United States to mediate a resolution to rebellion
  - Spain did not heed ultimatum; United States declared war April 25, 1898

- results:
  - Cuba freed

- Teller Amendment (1898) pledged the United States would not acquire Cuba
- Platt Amendment (1901) said Cuba must clear all treaties with United States
- United States acquired Puerto Rico, Guam, and the Philippine Islands
- United States paid Spain $20 million
- political/diplomatic impact:
  - war did resolve the Cuban conflict, but Cuba eluded clear American acquisition
  - United States joined the march for empire
  - United States became a colonial, imperialist power
  - United States became very aggressive in Caribbean

Long Essay Question 10

Compare and contrast the successes and failures of the abolitionist and women's movements in expanding democracy in the nineteenth century.

(POL-2; Comparison and Contrast; Lessons 11, 20, 21)

Students can use a variety of facts and ideas to answer this prompt. In addition to the information in Lessons 11, 20, and 21, your students could include:

OVERALL THEMES

1. The two movements were closely related, many women reformers receiving their training and experience in the abolitionist movement.

2. The abolitionists achieved their primary goal when the Thirteenth Amendment ended slavery in 1865.

3. Women did not have the same successes. Between 1848 and 1865, women subordinated their efforts to the antislavery cause.

4. After the Civil War, the women's suffrage movement divided over the Fifteenth Amendment and the question of African-American male suffrage.

5. At the end of the century, women were still without their primary goal—suffrage.

POSSIBLE INFORMATION

Abolitionist Movement

- William Lloyd Garrison:
  - led abolitionists 1831–1865
  - began publishing The Liberator 1831
  - helped found the American Anti-Slavery Society 1833
  - very controversial

- many fellow abolitionists thought him rancorous and abusive
- he called for:
  » immediate abolition of slavery
  » no compensation for owners
  » attacks on the churches for not speaking out against slavery
  » attacked the Constitution—called it a pact with the devil
  » active and equal role for women in the movement
- by 1838 American Anti-Slavery Society claimed to have 250,000 members
- Garrison was always opposed to political action—he wanted slavery ended through moral persuasion
- Lewis and Arthur Tappan
  - allies of Garrison in early 1830s, broke with him in 1840
  - formed American and Foreign Anti-Slavery Society
  - called for:
    » gradual emancipation
    » compensation to owners
    » political action—supported Liberty Party, later Free Soil Party
    » alliance with churches
    » women must accept a secondary and inferior role in the movement
- by early 1850s, Society was in trouble and faded in mid-1850s
- impact of abolitionists:
  - insisted the North choose between principles of antislavery and the Union
  - South believed abolitionists would bring on a "holocaust of blood"
  - many northerners did not like being forced to think about slavery
  - helped to bring on the Civil War
  - achieved their goal of ending slavery

The Women's Movement

1848–1865

- women were active in temperance and abolition crusade before the Civil War
- diluted their work for suffrage
- William Lloyd Garrison very influential—he suggested:
  - the principle of absolute human equality
  - the theory of social change: must change people's hearts and ideas as well as laws
- The Liberator had a "Ladies Department"—issues for and about women
- in 1830s, women formed several female antislavery societies
- women's role in the abolitionist movement became a flash point of controversy between Garrison and his supporters
- Seneca Falls Convention:
  - organized by Elizabeth Cady Stanton, Lucretia Mott

- ○ held July 19–20, 1848
- ○ 300 participants (40 men)
- ○ issued Declaration of Sentiments
- ○ first demand was for the right to vote
- women's rights activists held an annual convention from 1848 to the beginning of the Civil War (except in 1857)
- in 1840s and 1850s made progress in getting fairer divorce laws for women, right to own property and keep wages
- during Civil War, women organized the Woman's Loyal National League
  - ○ worked for Union and emancipation

1865–1900

- women divided over Fifteenth Amendment
- leaders like Susan B. Anthony and Elizabeth Stanton wanted women included in Fifteenth Amendment
- others like Lucy Stone and Julia Ward Howe said women should wait—it was the Negro's hour
- rival organizations evolved from this dispute
  - ○ American Woman Suffrage Association, 1869
    - » leader Lucy Stone
    - » accepted Fifteenth Amendment as it was
    - » worked at state level for women's suffrage
    - » focused on the suffrage exclusively
    - » more conservative—accepted "cult of true womanhood"
  - ○ National Woman Suffrage Association, 1868
    - » leaders Anthony and Stanton
    - » demanded Fifteenth Amendment include women as well as black men
    - » more aggressive, militant—only women allowed to be officers
- became increasingly antiblack in rhetoric
- 1890 two groups combined into National American Woman Suffrage Association
- Elizabeth Cady Stanton first president
- tended to diminish the role of the American Woman Suffrage group
- some states gave women suffrage—Colorado, Idaho, Wyoming—but no national right to vote achieved
- 1875 Minor v. Happersett ruled that suffrage was not attached to women's citizenship
- summary: although women made speeches, tried to vote, and staged demonstrations, they failed to achieve their overarching nineteenth-century goal of suffrage

Long Essay Question 11

Evaluate the extent to which Congress and the Supreme Court helped the South win the peace after the Civil War.

Consider the years 1868–1900.

(NAT-2, POL-3; Causation; Lessons 23, 24)

Students can use a variety of facts and ideas to answer this prompt. In addition to the information in Lessons 23 and 24, your students could include some of the following ideas:

OVERALL THEMES

1. Congress began to lose interest in Reconstruction after 1868.

2. The failure to convict Andrew Johnson and the death of Thaddeus Stevens in 1868 undermined Radical Republican reformers in Congress.

3. The election dispute in 1876 set the stage for an end to Congressional reconstruction of the South.

4. The Supreme Court began to shrink the legal impact of the Fourteenth Amendment in the early 1870s.

5. From 1873–1896, the Court issued a series of rulings that strengthened the rights of the states to enforce laws within their boundaries.

6. The Court restricted the federal government's authority to involve itself in cases of private discrimination.

7. The Court found the Fourteenth Amendment did not require integrated facilities for races, only required they be equal in quality.

POSSIBLE INFORMATION

Congressional Role

- Johnson's impeachment
  - the failure to convict Andrew Johnson for his violation of the Tenure of Office Act in 1868 weakened the Radical Republicans
  - Thaddeus Stevens' death further hurt the goal of transforming the South
- Grant's presidency
  - Grant wanted peace, and he did not challenge Congress on the gradual return to power of southern conservative redeemers
  - Panic of 1873 focused nation's attention on economic issues rather than civil rights
  - Grant scandals crowded other issues from national agenda

- Compromise of 1877
  - in order to get Rutherford B. Hayes certified as president, northern Republicans withdrew troops from the last southern states
  - left South to restore its economic and social system
  - showed that the nation was ready to put war behind it and wanted
  - reconciliation
  - "The hour of the Negro had passed"
  - Reconstruction was over
- Hayes's presidency featured reconciliation with the South
  - no attempt to enforce statutes protecting civil rights
  - desire to heal the sectional wounds of the war

The Supreme Court

- Court followed government's overall philosophy of returning power to southern states and reconciling North with South
- In Slaughterhouse cases, *U.S. v. Cruikshank, Reese v. U.S., U.S. v. Singleton,* Court established that:
  - citizenship rights should be protected at state level
  - protection of rights to assemble and bear arms would remain state
  - responsibility
  - federal government could prevent only cases of state-sponsored
  - discrimination; could not intervene in cases of private bias
  - paved way for *Plessy v. Ferguson* (1896)
- Court rejected centralizing tendencies of the Fourteenth Amendment
- Struck down Civil Rights Act of 1875 in Singleton case (1883)
- *Plessy v. Ferguson*
  - upheld Jim Crow system in railroads
  - allowed separate facilities as long as they were equal
  - Court also ruled/implied:
    » Fourteenth Amendment did not abolish all distinction based on race
    » government could not force social integration
    » government cannot put blacks on same social plane as whites
    » separation is badge of inferiority only if blacks interpret it that way
    » "law ways cannot change folkways"
    » laid foundation for entire Jim Crow system

Long Essay Question 12

Analyze the main issues that framed the debate over the appropriate role of the federal government in the American economy from 1880–1910.

(POL-3; Change over Time; Lessons 25, 26, 28)

Students can use a variety of facts and ideas to answer this prompt. In addition to the information in Lessons 25, 26, and 28, your students could include some of the following:

OVERALL THEMES

1. Main struggle between the forces supporting government intervention and the forces of laissez-faire.

2. Social Darwinist and their ideas dominated the late 19th century economic discussion.

3. According to Social Darwinists the proper role of the government was to protect private property and avoid upsetting the natural order of unbridled competition.

4. Reformers called for more government regulation to achieve a balanced social and economic order.

5. Government in the Progressive Era became active in regulating the environment and the consumer market place.

6. The Supreme Court tended to limit government actions in the economy from 1880–1910.

7. The currency issue faded after McKinley election victory in 1896.

8. From 1880–1900 the government tried to address the currency issue by purchasing and coining limited amount of silver.

POSSIBLE INFORMATION

Social Darwinists

- followed the writing of Herbert Spencer and William Graham Sumner
- warned against government intervention and interference with social and economic evolution
- believed helping poor impeded progress in United States
- believed the gold standard was the best for the economy
- applauded Supreme Court rulings such as E.C Knight and Lochner, which limited the government's power to regulate the economic system
- believed the poor were responsible for their fate

Reform Darwinists (Social Gospel Members)

- believed freedom and spiritual self-development required equalization of wealth and power
- believed unbridled competition mocked Christian ideals of brotherhood

- drew inspiration from writers such as Walter Rauschenbusch, Lyman Abbot
- did not take a strong position on the currency question

Progressive Reformers

- drew inspiration from writers such Henry George, Edward Bellamy, Henry Demarest Lloyd
- reformer Presidents included Theodore Roosevelt, William Howard Taft, Woodrow Wilson
- used Sherman Act, Hepburn Act, Mann Elkins Act to control corporations
- supported Supreme Court rulings in Northern Securities Case, *Muller v. Oregon*
- enacted laws to regulate child labor
- called for a "Square Deal" for laboring people and the middle class
- believed freedom was the power of the government to act on behalf of the people
- rooted out corruption with initiative, recall, and referendum

Long Essay Question 13

Compare and contrast the role of TWO civil rights leaders in combating the Jim Crow system from 1890-1925.

(POL-2; Comparison and Contrast; Lesson 27)

Students can use a variety of facts and ideas to answer this prompt. In addition to the information in Lesson 27, your students could include:

OVERALL THEMES

1. Great struggle between Booker T. Washington and W.E.B. Du Bois to lead African Americans against Jim Crow.

2. Washington called for accommodation and some acceptance of the Jim Crow system. He emphasized economic advancement for African Americans rather than social and political agitation.

3. Washington favored acceptance of the racial status quo from 1895–1915.

4. Du Bois emphasized agitation and immediate changes.

5. Du Bois called for full equality and the dismantling of the entire Jim Crow system.

6. Marcus Garvey was closer to Washington in philosophy in his call for economic progress to lead to a better quality of life. He also accepted segregation in many aspects of black life. Yet, his separatist, back-to-Africa ideas placed him in a more radical position than either Washington or Du Bois.

POSSIBLE INFORMATION

Booker T. Washington

- born a slave, grew up in South
- educated at Hampton Institute
- ceased to have "bitterness against southern whites"
- became president of Tuskegee Institute
- gained national prominence in 1895 with his "Atlanta Compromise" speech which:
  - emphasized economic issues
  - said blacks SHOULD NOT:
    - run from work; rather they should embrace it
    - worry about political rights
    - agitate on social questions
    - let grievances overshadow economic opportunities
    - seek social equality—remain as "separate as fingers on a hand" from white people
  - said blacks SHOULD:
    - cast down economic buckets where they were and work hard for white acceptance
    - live by the production of their hands
    - obtain training in agriculture and trades
    - do right and the world would be all right
    - accept conditions as they now exist
- Washington received support from white industrialists
  - George Eastman gave $10,000 annually to Tuskegee
  - John D. Rockefeller gave $10,000 as well
  - Andrew Carnegie added $600,000 to Tuskegee endowment, 1903
- Washington became influential leader with political and economic connections throughout the white world
- criticism:
  - no real progress made by blacks—whites still discriminated and held blacks back
  - his don't-rock-the-boat policies made him seem like an "Uncle Tom"
  - did not challenge whites and the Jim Crow system
  - deeply hurt by the Atlanta Riot and Brownsville Raid in 1906
- secretly worked behind the scenes to try to tear down Jim Crow

W.E.B. Du Bois

- born after the Civil War in Massachusetts
- never a slave, grew up in Massachusetts
- earned Ph.D. from Harvard in 1895
- at first supported Washington's position on Jim Crow

- broke with Washington in 1903 with publication of his book The Souls of Black Folk
- founding member of the Niagara Movement and the National Association for the Advancement of Colored People (NAACP)
- taught at several southern colleges
- said: "the problem of the twentieth century is the problem of the color line"
- called for:
  - direct assault on the Jim Crow system
  - black agitation for all social, political, and economic benefits that America offered to white people
  - putting responsibility for racial solutions on white people not blacks
  - the "Talented Tenth" of the black community to lead the charge for equal rights (educated people like DuBois and his friends)
  - blacks should study liberal arts and seek professional education opportunities
- critics said he:
  - was out of touch with average black people
  - did not know the South
  - was an elitist
- eventually he broke with the NAACP
- more and more critical of America and capitalism
- in 1950s and 1960s, left country and joined the Communist Party

Marcus Garvey

- came to United States from Jamaica in 1916 to get support from Booker T. Washington
- connected with urban, poor African Americans
- message:
  - black pride
  - blacks should seek African roots
  - economic self-sufficiency
  - seek lands where blacks were in the majority—Africa
  - motto: "One God, One Aim, One Destiny"
  - blacks should follow separate course of economic advancement
- strongly promoted cultural, economic links with Africa
- founded the Universal Negro Improvement Association (UNIA)
- created the Black Star Line—black-owned shipping company
- founded the Negro Factory Corporation
- tried to connect the UNIA with Liberia
- criticized NAACP and Du Bois as outdated and too close to whites
- arrested in 1922 for mail fraud
- deported in 1927
- criticism:

- ○ his separatist message was actually endorsed by the Ku Klux Klan
- ○ his elaborate costumes and flamboyant behaviors were ridiculed by many people
- ○ his fraud represented his betrayal of the thousands of blacks who had invested in his economic schemes

Long Essay Question 14

Evaluate the extent to which political and economic reform movements promoted social justice in the United States from 1900–1940.

Consider at least TWO movements.

(POL-2; Change over Time and Causation; Lessons 8, 9, 29, 31)

Students can use a variety of facts and ideas to answer this prompt. In addition to the information in Lessons 8, 9, 29, and 31, your students could include:

OVERALL THEMES

1. Social justice refers to equal access to due process and equal opportunity to society's bounty and riches regardless of gender, class, religion, ethnicity, or race.

2. The economic reforms of the Progressives (1901–1917) and the New Dealers (1933–1939) placed the government on the side of the middle class and against special and powerful interests.

3. In both cases, government actions involved business regulation, taxing the rich, and reducing barriers to economic advancement.

4. Both movements had limited success in changing the economic and political structure and improving conditions for the middle class and working poor.

5. However, both movements began the march to a fairer, more equal America.

POSSIBLE INFORMATION

Square Deal and New Freedom Actions

- regulation of corporations
  - ○ Theodore Roosevelt, William Howard Taft, and Woodrow Wilson brought 214 suits against corporations from 1902–1917 under the Sherman Antitrust Act
  - ○ Congress passed:
    - » Hepburn Act (1906)—expanded Interstate Commerce Commission
    - » Elkins Act (1904)—outlawed railroad rebates
    - » Mann-Elkins Act (1910)—further regulated railroads
    - » Clayton Antitrust Act (1914)—regulated trusts, unfair competition
    - » Federal Trade Commission (1914)—outlawed unfair trade practices

» Federal Reserve Act (1913)—regulated banking industry
- citizen protection
  ○ Pure Food and Drug Act (1906)
  ○ Meat Inspection Act (1906)
  ○ Keating-Owen Act (1916)—prohibited the interstate shipment of goods
  ○ manufactured by firms employing children under fourteen years old
  ○ created Children's Bureau within Department of Labor
- Sixteenth Amendment enacted (1913)—an income tax that required the rich to pay at least partially for maintaining government services
- Progressives made business more cautious, and offered some protection and services to the middle class
- progressives supported the movement that eventually resulted in the Nineteenth Amendment granting women's suffrage
- failed to alter the unequal distribution of power and wealth in the country
- did not address the inequality of the Jim Crow system
- did not provide welfare payments to the poor and those unable to work

New Deal Actions

- FDR used the Three Rs—relief, recovery, and reform—to promote limited social justice in the 1930s
- the New Deal built on the progressive tradition of Theodore Roosevelt and Woodrow Wilson
- through a series of programs, the New Deal assisted the forgotten people of the middle class
  ○ Agricultural Adjustment Act—helped farmers
  ○ Emergency Relief Act—provided money for direct relief
  ○ many work programs (WPA, CWA, PWA, CCC)—created temporary jobs for the unemployed
  ○ Glass-Steagall Act—regulated banks and set up the Federal Deposit Insurance Corporation
  ○ Security and Exchange Commission—regulated Wall Street and stock market
- Roosevelt's Second New Deal confronted businesses and the rich, and tried to assist workers, the middle class, and the poor
  ○ Holding Company Act—designed to break up the utility holding companies
  ○ Revenue Act—higher taxes on rich
  ○ Wagner Act—made unionizing easier for workers
  ○ Social Security Act—government-mandated retirement system
- Roosevelt made permanent changes in the country's attitude toward government intervention on behalf of farmers, unionized workers, and small businessmen
- New Deal indirectly helped African Americans and won their votes, but Roosevelt did not propose a civil rights program
- nor did the New Deal directly help women, although Eleanor Roosevelt was an

active and vocal proponent for women's rights; Molly Dewson headed the Women's Division of the Democratic National Committee, which helped women obtain federal appointments in the government

- summary: New Deal did promote social justice by empowering new interest groups and allowing them to compete more effectively in the market

Long Essay Question 15

Evaluate the extent to which American foreign policy from 1920–1941 maintained continuity as well as promoted change in America's view of itself in world affairs.

(WOR-2; Continuity and Change; Lessons 22, 30)

Students can use a variety of facts and ideas to answer this prompt. In addition to the information found in Lessons 22 and 30, your students could include:

OVERALL THEMES

1. After rejecting membership in the League of Nations, the United States returned to its classic policy of avoiding entangling political and military alliances with Europe.

2. During these years, the United States practiced economic isolationism by maintaining high tariffs, immigration restrictions, and inflexible war debt policies.

3. During the 1920s, however, the nation did initiate and sign a series of international disarmament treaties.

4. The onset of the Great Depression reinforced the nation's determination to avoid Europe's military and political turmoil.

5. When World War II began in Europe, the United States realized its security was threatened, so it abandoned its policy of neutrality and isolation.

POSSIBLE INFORMATION

1920–1933

- U.S. refused to join the League of Nations and World Court
- U.S. practiced economic isolationism
  - restricted immigration—number of immigrants declined from 800,000 in 1920 to 150,000 in 1929
  - refused to offer forgiveness or flexibility on payments of $20 billion in war debts owed by Europe
  - maintained high tariffs
    - » Fordney-McCumber 1922
    - » Hawley-Smoot 1930
  - U.S. did, however, involve itself in a series of multinational disarmament treaties

with Europe and Japan

» Washington Conference (1921)—naval reduction, ten-year moratorium on battleship construction

» Five-Power Pact (1922)—established ratios for naval building

» Kellogg-Briand Pact (1928)—outlawed war as a means of settling international disputes

1933–1939

- Roosevelt, although an internationalist, was more concerned about the domestic Depression than world developments

- FDR did lower tariffs through Reciprocal Trade Agreement Act of 1934

- Isolationists controlled legislative agenda

  ◦ 1935–1937 passed a series of Neutrality Acts that called for:

    » mandatory arms embargo

    » restriction of Americans' travel on belligerent ships

    » prohibition on loans to belligerents

    » cash-and-carry for all exports in time of war

    » as historian Thomas Bailey said about the Neutrality Acts: "In retrospect, the United States was one war too late in its attempt to legislate itself into neutrality"

- Roosevelt was unable to use the Panay incident or his quarantine speech (both in 1937) to move the nation toward a strong international stance

1939–1941

- When war broke out in September 1939 in Europe, the United States began to dismantle its neutrality policy

  ◦ November 1939 repealed the arms embargo

  ◦ September 1940 established conscription

  ◦ September 1940 made destroyer-for-bases deal with England

  ◦ January 1941 enacted Lend-Lease

- undeclared shooting war on the seas between the U.S. and Germany brought America to the brink of war by autumn 1941

- U.S. economic pressure on Japan and the continued stalemate over the Japanese invasion of China led to Japanese attack on Pearl Harbor in December 7, 1941

- December 10, 1941, Germany declared war on U.S.

Long Essay Question 16

Some historians have suggested that private individuals rather than political figures played a greater role in promoting civil rights after World War II.

Support, modify, or refute this interpretation providing specific evidence from the contributions of at least two individuals from 1945–1969 to justify your answer.

(POL-2; Causation; Lessons 27, 32)

Students can use a variety of facts and ideas to answer this prompt. In addition to the information found in Lessons 27 and 32, your students could include:

OVERALL THEMES

1. Truman was the first president to put a true civil rights program on the legislative agenda.

2. Lyndon Johnson's War on Poverty included a strong civil rights component.

3. Johnson was the greatest presidential leader for civil rights in the twentieth century.

4. Martin Luther King Jr. was the most influential civil rights leader in America from 1956–1968.

5. During the early and mid-1960s, Malcolm X and other militant leaders began to challenge and question King's effectiveness and strategies.

POSSIBLE INFORMATION

Harry Truman

- became concerned about civil rights because of the treatment of black soldiers returning to America after World War II

- saw the glaring hypocrisy of fighting to stamp out Fascist racism around the world and perpetuating racism at home

- December 1946 appointed Civil Rights Committee; their report To Secure These Rights became core of Truman's program

- June 1947 became first president to address the NAACP

- July 1948 issued Executive Orders 9980 and 9981
  - 9980: integrated the federal work force
  - 9981: integrated U.S. armed forces

- during election campaign of 1948 called for:
  - creating civil rights division in Department of Justice
  - permanent commission on civil rights
  - Fair Employment Practices Commission
  - end to the poll tax

- end to discrimination in interstate transportation
- home rule/suffrage for the District of Columbia
- statehood for Alaska and Hawaii
- settlement of Japanese-American evacuation claims from WW II
- split his party in election of 1948
- Truman could not get Congress to act on most of his proposals, but he led the way in awakening nation's conscience on civil rights

Martin Luther King Jr.

- came to prominence in December 1955 with the Montgomery Bus Boycott
  - spokesman for the cause
  - when Supreme Court required Montgomery bus system to abandon Jim Crow in November 1956, King came into the national spotlight
- organized 30,000 people to come to Lincoln Memorial May 17, 1957
- founded the Southern Christian Leadership Conference (SCLC)
  - called for nonviolent coercion to achieve goals
  - used public protests to pressure whites to dismantle Jim Crow system
- supported but did not start the sit-ins and the freedom rides of the early 1960s
- came to true national prominence in spring of 1963
  - organized the protest against segregation in Birmingham, Alabama
  - arrested and wrote his famous "Letter from Birmingham Jail"
    - » emphasized direct action
    - » said cup of endurance and forbearance was overflowing for blacks
    - » blamed white moderates for slow pace of racial change
    - » also criticized the churches for inaction
- violence in Birmingham pressured President Kennedy to propose a civil rights act in June of 1963
- King organized march to lobby the president and Congress to approve the act
  - initially, march was to feature civil disobedience
  - Kennedy administration opposed this
  - 250,000 who joined King at Lincoln Memorial heard his "I Have a Dream" speech
  - high point of King's influence
  - 1963 fully 88 percent of blacks supported King's effort
- Civil Rights Act passed July 1964
- King won Nobel Peace Prize in 1964
- urban rioting began in 1964 and started to erode King's support
- Selma protest led to Voting Rights Act of 1965
- urban riots increased violence, gave rise to militancy of Student Nonviolent Coordinating Committee and individuals such as Malcolm X
- 1967 King criticized war in Vietnam

- ◦ King said U.S. is greatest purveyor of violence in world
- ◦ Johnson felt betrayed
- 1968 under increasing pressure from radicals
- April 1968 assassinated in Memphis, Tennessee

Lyndon Johnson

- although a southerner, he had a moderate record on civil rights as a legislator
  - ◦ one of three southern Senators who refused to sign the southern manifesto of resistance to the Brown v. Board of Education decision in 1957
  - ◦ helped pass Civil Rights Acts of 1957 and 1960
- as president, declared a War on Poverty, which included civil rights programs
- achievements:
  - ◦ Civil Rights Act of 1964—most far-reaching civil rights law since Reconstruction
  - ◦ Voting Rights Act of 1965—voting rights, changed the political face of the South
  - ◦ 1964 created Equal Employment Opportunity Commission—investigated and prevented job discrimination
  - ◦ 1965 Immigration Act—revised 1924 quota system
  - ◦ Congress enacted food stamp program and public housing assistance
  - ◦ Congress passed sixty bills providing aid to education, 1964–1969
  - ◦ riots and Vietnam War undermined his program
    - » in 1964, rioting starts in cities
    - » in 1966, 128 cities had some type of disorder
    - » in 1967, 164 cities had riots
- summary: greatest civil rights record in history of the country

Malcolm X

- member of the (Black) Muslims of America
- criticized the nonviolent, integration approach of Martin Luther King Jr.
- opposed:
  - ◦ integration—he asked: Why integrate with a burning house?
  - ◦ March on Washington in 1963
    - » called it the "Farce on Washington"
    - » said it was controlled by white power structure
    - » said blacks could not end racism by holding hands and singing songs
- called for:
  - ◦ black self-defense
  - ◦ realization that whites were the devil
  - ◦ racial pride and unity
  - ◦ projection of black manhood
- had some influence with undereducated, unemployed urban black males
- broke with Elijah Muhammad over Muhammad's personal behavior

- claimed his trip to Mecca in 1964 softened his antiwhite beliefs
- assassinated in 1965 by another faction of Muslims
- on fringes of the civil rights movement; in 1965 only 5 percent of blacks said he was doing the best job on their behalf

Long Essay Question 17

Compare and contrast the successes and failures of containment of TWO Cold War presidents from 1945-1974.

(WOR-2; Compare and Contrast; Lessons 33, 34, 35)

Students can use a variety of facts and ideas to answer this prompt. In addition to the information in Lessons 33, 34, and 35, your students could include:

OVERALL THEMES

1. The concept of containment became America's overriding strategy throughout the Cold War.

2. Each president fine-tuned the implementation of the policy and labeled it differently, but all remained committed to its assumptions and overall strategy.

3. The concept of containment grew from the pre-World War II experiences of trying to appease totalitarianism in Europe and Asia.

4. American leaders came to see the Communists as "the new Nazis" who could not be allowed to seize territory incrementally.

5. The Vietnam War proved to be both the apex and the turning point in the implementation of containment.

POSSIBLE INFORMATION

Harry Truman

- based containment on ideas of George F. Kennan's "Long Telegram" and "Sources of Soviet Conduct"
- saw Soviets as expansionistic and threatening to American interests
- implementation of containment
  - Truman Doctrine (1947)—$400 million to help Greece and Turkey resist Communist guerrillas
  - Marshall Plan (1948–1951)—$12.5 billion to aid Europe
  - Berlin Air Lift (1948–1949)—supplied West Berlin for 324 days when it was threatened by Soviets
- North Atlantic Treaty Organization (1949)—military alliance with Western Europe to stop potential Soviet aggression

- NSC 68 (1950)—called for tripling the defense budget; putting country on a state-of-war readiness to prevent world domination by the Soviet Union
- Korean War (1950–1953)
- Truman outlined parameters of containment that all future presidents would largely follow
- U.S. committed to being "the world's policeman"

Dwight Eisenhower

- came to power calling for a "New Look" in foreign policy
- spokesman was Secretary of State John Foster Dulles
- viewed Communism as monolithic
- implementation of containment
    - massive retaliation—nuclear response to Communist aggression
    - no more limited wars like Korean conflict
    - take Soviets to brink of war if necessary to stop their aggression
    - rollback and liberate areas under Communist control
    - increased spending on atomic weapons, missiles, and bombers
    - gave Central Intelligence Agency broad power
    - called for "peaceful coexistence" with Soviets
    - proposed "domino theory" as justification to help Vietnam resist Communist aggression
    - used force in Middle East to keep out Communists (Eisenhower Doctrine)
- summary: while using different rhetoric, Eisenhower "traveled the well-rutted road" of containment

John Kennedy

- accepted basic outline of containment
- altered Eisenhower's massive retaliation with his "flexible response"—expanded options for fighting Communist threat
- focused on Berlin as great trouble spot and "wars of liberation" in Asia, Africa, and Latin America
- implementation of containment
    - April 1961 tried to overthrow Fidel Castro in Cuba—failed invasion at Bay of Pigs
- October 1962 confronted the Soviet Union and forced the removal of nuclear weapons from Cuba (Cuban Missile Crisis)
- accepted domino theory and deepened American commitment in Vietnam
    - sent 16,000 advisors to South Vietnam
    - November 1963 supported a coup that eliminated Ngo Dinh Diem—set off chaos in country and set stage for America's quagmire in Vietnam
- summary: Kennedy was a traditional cold warrior in mold of Truman and Eisenhower

Lyndon Johnson

- accepted basic ideas of Cold War and containment—believed communism:
    - was monolithic—controlled from Moscow
    - must be contained
    - threatened America's prestige as world power
- believed in domino theory and that Vietnam was critical to all of Southeast Asia's future
- remembered how Truman's presidency had been damaged by the fall of China to the Communists in 1949
- wanted to protect support for his domestic programs by being tough with Communists
- wanted to honor John Kennedy's memory
- reduced tension with Cuba and sought status quo in Europe with Communists
- faced crisis in Vietnam
    - death of Diem resulted in chaos throughout country
    - by 1964 estimated that 40 percent of land and 50 percent of people in South Vietnam were controlled by Communists
    - Gulf of Tonkin Resolution gave him a blank check to wage war in Vietnam
- eventually sent 540,000 troops to South Vietnam and heavily bombed North Vietnam
- war divided the nation and destroyed Johnson's presidency
- Vietnam showed the limits of containment and of America's ability to shape the world
- summary: country began to question the assumptions and reality of being the world's police force

Richard Nixon

- although committed to broad outline of containment, Nixon began to redefine the concept
- realized United States must disengage in Vietnam
- saw great opportunity for United States with the rivalry between the Soviet Union and China for control of the international Communist movement
- Nixon dropped idea that Communism was monolithic
- Nixon realized the United States must remain a world power, but must rethink its international approach
- Nixon and Henry Kissinger tried to construct a new global strategy with less emphasis on traditional containment:
    - Vietnamization in Vietnam—withdraw combat troops but pressure Communists to negotiate a settlement
    - use tension between the USSR and China to America's strategic advantage
        - » Nixon visited China in February 1972
        - » United States offered China American technology
        - » signed a Strategic Arms Limitations Treaty (SALT) with Soviet Union
    - looked for peaceful coexistence and cooperation (détente) with Soviet Union

- wound down war in Vietnam
    - » June 1969 withdrew 25,000 troops from Vietnam
    - » 1970–1972 continued to pull American troops out and tried to force Communists to negotiate for peace
  - 1973 ended draft
  - 1973 withdrew last American troops and signed peace accord
- supported containment of Communist power, but hoped the carrot-and-stick approach would transform both countries into more traditional powers
- summary: the Watergate scandal short-circuited Nixon/Kissinger's vision of a new phase of containment

Document-Based Questions

with Suggested Responses

QUESTION 1: EMERGING COLONIAL IDENTITY

Analyze the changes in the political structure and social fabric in British North America from 1620–1680 that promoted an emerging colonial identity.

(NAT-1; Continuity/Change and Historical Causation)

Document 1

Source: The introduction of African slavery into the American colonies at Jamestown, Virginia, August, 1619

INTRODUCTION OF SLAVERY.

Document 2

Source: The Mayflower Compact, 1620

…We whose names are underwritten … do by these presents solemnly and mutually in the presence of God, and one of another, covenant and combine ourselves together into a civil body politics for our better ordering and preservation and furtherance of the ends aforesaid; and by virtue hereof, to enact, constitute, and frame such just and equal laws, ordinances, acts, constitutions, and offices from time to time, as shall be thought most meet and convenient for the general good of the colony unto which we promise all due submission and obedience…

Document 3

Source: Roger Williams, 1644

Sixth. It is the will and command of God that since the coming of his Son, the Lord Jesus a permission of the most pagan, Jewish, Turkish, or anti-Christian consciences and worships be granted to all men in all nations and countries…

Eighth. God requires not a uniformity of religion to be enacted and enforced in any civil state…enforced uniformity…is the greatest occasion of civil war, ravishing of conscience, persecution of Christ Jesus in his servants, and of the hypocrisy and destruction of millions of souls.

Twelfth. …the Church of Christ does not used the arm of secular power to compel men to the true profession of the truth, for this is to be done with spiritual weapons, whereby Christians are to be exhorted, not compelled.

Document 4

Source: Navigation Acts, 1660

I.   For the increase of shipping and encouragement of the navigation of this nation wherein, under the good providence and protection of God, the wealth, safety, and strength of this kingdom is so much concerned; be it enacted by the king's most excellent Majesty,...no goods or commodities whatsoever shall be imported into or exported out of any lands, islands, plantations, or territories to his Majesty...in any other ship or ships, vessel or vessels whatsoever, but in such ships as do truly and without fraud belong only to the people of England or Ireland....

II.   And be it enacted, that no alien or person not born within the allegiance of our sovereign lord the king...[shall] exercise the trade or occupation of a merchant or factor in any the said place;

Document 5

Source: Increase Mather, 1675

August 12. This is the memorable day wherein Philip, the perfidious and bloudy [sic] Author of the War and wofull miseryes [sic] that have thence ensued, was taken and slain. And God brought it to pass, chiefly by Indians themselves,....Divine Providence so disposed....The Indian who thus killed Philip did formerly belong to the Squaw-Sachim of Pocasset, ...Thus when Philip had made an end to deal treacherously, his own Subjects dealt treacherously with him.... [Philip was] taken and destroyed, and there was he cut into four quarters, and is now hanged up as a monument of revenging justice, his head being cut off and carried away to Plymouth ....

Document 6

Source: Nathaniel Bacon's Declaration, 1676

1. For having, upon specious pretenses of public works, raised great unjust taxes upon the commonalty for the advancement of private favorites and other sinister end, but no visible effects in any measure adequate; for not having, during this long time of his government, in any measure this hopeful colony either by fortifications, towns, or trade.

4. For having protected, favored, and emboldened the Indians against his Majesty's loyal subjects, never contriving, requiring, or appointing any due or proper means of satisfaction for their many invasions, robberies, and murders committed upon us.

8. For the prevention of civil mischief and ruin amongst ourselves while the barbarous enemy in all places did invade, murder, and spoil us, his Majesty's most faithful subjects.

Of this and the aforesaid articles we accuse Sir William Berkeley [royal governor] as guilty of each and every one of the same…

Document 7

Source: Poem by Anne Bradstreet from her collection, Several Poems Compiled with Great Variety of Wit and Learning, 1678, published posthumously by her family

To my Dear and Loving Husband
If ever two were one, then surely we.
If ever man were lov'd by wife, then thee.
If ever wife was happy in a man,
Compare with me, ye women, if you can.
I prize they love more than whole Mines of gold
Or all the riches that the East doth hold.
My love is such that Rivers canneot [sic] quench,
Nor ought but love from thee give recompetence.
Thy love is such I can no way repay.
The heavens reward thee manifold, I pray.
Then while we live, in love let's so persever [sic]
That when we live no more, we may live ever.

Suggested Elements of an Emerging Colonial Identity

The colonists saw themselves from 1620–1680 as a people who:

- wrote down their rules of government in compacts and charters
- valued their rights as Englishmen even in the colonies
- practiced some degree of religious freedom
- were responsible to the Crown and its rules
- solved their labor problems by enslaving Africans
- felt superior to Africans and Native Americans
- justified harsh treatment of Native Americans when they resisted colonial actions
- would not accept abridgment of their rights as Englishmen
- valued marriage, family life
- saw men as superior to women in society
- accepted gender roles of women's subservience to men in colonial life

QUESTION 2: WOMEN'S RIGHTS, 1848–1870

How did the strategies and supporters in the crusade for the rights of women change from 1848–1872? What factors account for this evolution in approach and personnel?

(POL-2; Continuity/Change, Historical Causation,
& Use of Relevant Historical Evidence)

Document 1

Source: Proceedings from Woman's Rights Convention, Seneca Falls, New York, July 19-21, 1848

We hold these truths to be self-evident: all men and women are created equal; that they are endowed by their Creator with certain inalienable rights; that among these are life, liberty and the pursuit of happiness; that to secure these rights governments are instituted, deriving their just powers from the consent of the governed…The history of mankind is a history of repeated injuries and usurpations on the part of man toward woman, having in direct object the establishment of absolute tyranny over her.

Document 2

Source: Letter, Susan B. Anthony to Amelia Bloomer, August 26, 1852

Dear Mrs. Bloomer:

...I attended the great Temperance demonstration held at Albion, July 7...
I talked to them in my plain way,—told them that to merely relieve the
suffering wives and children of drunkards, and vainly labor to reform the
drunkard was no longer to be called temperance work, and showed them
that woman's temperance sentiments were not truthfully represented by
man at the Ballot Box...

...Men may prate on, but we women are beginning to know that the life
and happiness of a woman is of equal value with that of a man; and that
for a woman to sacrifice her health, happiness and perchance her earthly
existence in the hope of reclaiming a drunken, sensualized man, avails
but little ... Auxiliary Temperance Societies have been formed in very
nearly all the towns I have visited and the women are beginning to feel
that they have something to do in the Temperance Cause—that woman
may speak and act in public as well as in the home circle—and now is
the time to inscribe upon our banner, "NO UNION WITH DISTILLERS,
RUMSELLERS, AND RUMDRINKERS."

Yours for Temperance
without Compromise,

S. B. Anthony

Document 3

Source: Cartoon of the Ninth National Woman's Rights Convention, May 12, 1859

Document 4

Source: Address by Elizabeth Cady Stanton to the American Anti-Slavery Society, May 8, 1860

But in settling the question of negro's rights, we find out the exact limits of our own, for rights never clash or interfere; and where no individual in a community is denied his rights the mass are the more perfectly protected in theirs ... so the humblest and most ignorant citizen cannot be denied his rights without deranging the whole system of government.

I have always regarded Garrison [William Lloyd] as the great missionary of the gospel of Jesus to this guilty nation, for he has waged an uncompromising warfare with the deadly sins of both Church and State. ... In the darkness and gloom of a false theology, I was slowly sawing off the chains of my spiritual bondage, when, for the first time, I met Garrison in London; a few bold strokes from the hammer of his truth, I was free ... To Garrison we owe more than to any other man of our day...

Document 5

Source: Minutes, Women's Loyal National League Meeting, May 14, 1863

We the undersigned, Women of the United States, agree to become members of the Women's Loyal National League, ...

Resolved, That for the present this League will concentrate all its efforts upon the single object of procuring to be signed by one million women and upward, and of preparing for presentation to Congress, within the first week of its session, a petition in the following words to wit:

To the Senate and House of Representatives of the United States.

The undersigned, women of the United States about the age of 18 years, earnestly pray that your honorable body will pass, at the earliest practicable day, an act emancipating all persons of African descent held to involuntary service or labor in the United States.

Document 6

Source: Report, Eleventh National Woman's Rights Convention, May 10, 1866

Whereas, By the act of Emancipation and the Civil Rights bill, the negro and woman now hold the same civil and political status, alike needing only the ballot; and whereas the same arguments apply equally to both classes, proving all partial legislation to republican institutions, therefore...

...we have looked to State action only for the recognition of our rights; but now, by the results of the war, the whole question of suffrage reverts back to Congress and the Constitution. The duty of Congress at this moment is to declare what shall be the basis of representation in a republican form of government ... We, therefore, wish to broaden our Woman's Rights platform, and make it in name—what it ever has been in spirit—a Human Rights platform.

Document 7

Source: Speech, Frederick Douglass, American Equal Rights Convention, May 12, 1869

With us [the black man], the matter is a question of life and death, at least, in fifteen States of the Union. When women, because they are women, are hunted down through ... New York and New Orleans; when they are dragged from their houses and hung upon lampposts; when their children are torn from their arms, and their brains dashed out upon the pavement; when they are objects of insult and outrage at every turn; when they are in danger of having their homes burnt down over their heads; when their children are not allowed to enter schools; then they will have an urgency to obtain the ballot equal to our own.

Suggested Factors about Changes in Women's Rights, 1848–1870

Changing Strategy:

- held an annual meeting every year except 1857 from 1848-1861
- discussed their problems and inequalities at each convention
- joined in other reforms such as abolitionist and temperance
- during Civil War supported the union and emancipation
- after war wanted the 15th Amendment to include women
- some supporters said women should wait until black men were secure in the vote
- held conventions, wrote Congress after Civil War
- formed the National Women's Suffrage Association
- formed the American Women's Suffrage Association

Supporters:

- most men did not support the women's rights movement
- exceptions were men such as William Lloyd Garrison, Frederick Douglass
- Susan B. Anthony and Elizabeth Cady Stanton wanted women included in 15th Amendment (National Women's Suffrage Association)
- the drive to include women in the 15th Amendment alienated former supporters such as Frederick Douglass
- some women wanted to postpone women's suffrage until black men were accepted and secure in voting (American Women's Suffrage Association)
- the women's movement split after the Civil War over this issue

QUESTION 3: THE CHANGING ROLE OF GOVERNMENT, 1890–1912

Analyze the national government's changing philosophy and response to the nation's economic challenges from 1890–1912.

(POL-3; Continuity/Change, Historical Causation, & Use of Relevant Historical Evidence)

Document 1

Selective Categories of Employed Workers: 1880–1920

Year	Total Workers	Agriculture	Manu-facturing	Domestic Peronal Service	Government
1880	17,390,000	8,610,000	4,000,000	1,440,000	335,000
1890	23,740,000	9,990,000	6,190,000	2,160,000	360,000
1900	29,070,000	10,710,000	8,000,000	2,710,000	670,000
1910	36,730,000	11,340,000	10,530,000	3,670,000	1,140,000
1920	41,610,000	11,120,000	13,050,000	3,330,000	1,300,000

Document 2

Source: Sherman Act, 1890

Section 1. Every contract, combination in the form of trust or otherwise or conspiracy, in restraint of trade or commerce among the several States or with foreign nations, is hereby declared to be illegal...

Section 2. Every person who shall monopolize, or attempt to monopolize, or combine or conspire with any other person or persons, to monopolize any part of the trade or commerce among the several States, or with any foreign nations, shall be deemed guilty of a misdemeanor...

Document 3

> Source: Henry Demarest Lloyd, Wealth Against Commonwealth, 1894
>
> ...the syndicates, trusts, combinations cry of "overproduction"—too much of everything. Holding back the riches of earth, sea and sky from their fellows who famish and freeze in the dark, they declare to them that there is too much light and warmth and food. They assert the right, for their private profit, to regulate the consumption by the people of the necessaries of life, and to control production, not by the needs of humanity, but by the desires of a few for dividends ... The coal syndicate thinks there is too much coal. There is too much iron, too much lumber, too much flour—for this or that syndicate ...
>
> ...If the tendency to combination is irresistible, control of it is imperative. Monopoly and anti-monopoly ... represent the two great tendencies of our time: monopoly, the tendency to combination; anti-monopoly, the demand for social control of it.

Document 4

> Source: Jacob Coxey's proposal to Congress, June 12, 1894
>
> 1.　　The Good Roads Bill—53rd Congress, 2d Session H.R. 7438, June 12, 1894.
>
> A Bill to provide for the improvement of public roads and for other purposes.
>
> Be enacted by the Senate and the House of Representatives ... That the Secretary of Treasury of the United States is hereby authorized and instructed to have ... printed, immediately after the passage of this bill, five hundred million dollars of Treasury notes ... and to be placed in a fund to be known as the "general country-road fund system of the United States," and to be expended solely for said purpose.
>
> Section 2 That it shall be the duty of the Secretary of War to take charge of the construction of said general country-road system of the United States, and said construction to commerce as soon as the Secretary of Treasury shall inform the Secretary of War that the said fund is available ... it shall be the duty of the Secretary of War to inaugurate work and expend the sum of twenty millions of dollars per month pro rata with the number of miles of road in each State and Territory in the United States.

Document 5

Source: William Allen Rogers, Harper's Weekly, March 28, 1896

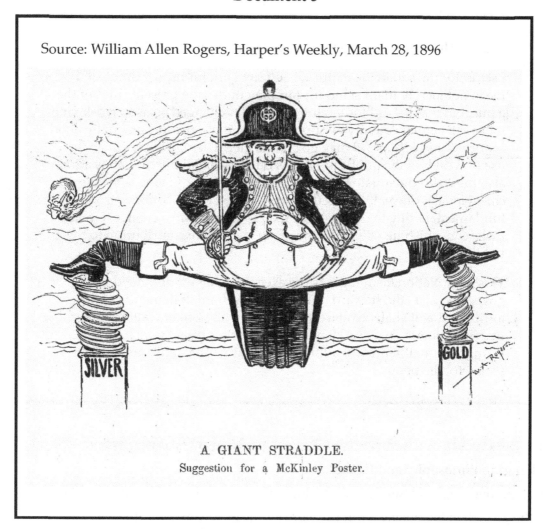

A GIANT STRADDLE.
Suggestion for a McKinley Poster.

Document 6

Source: *Lochner* v. *New York*, 1905

The statute necessarily interferes with the right of contract between the employer and employees, concerning the number of hours in which the latter may labor in the bakery of the employer. The general right to make a contract in relation to his business is part of the liberty of the individual protected by the Fourteenth Amendment of the Federal Constitution...

... The act ... is an illegal interference with the rights of individuals, both employers and employees, to make contracts regarding labor upon such terms as they may think best, or which they may agree upon with the other parties to such contracts. Statutes of the nature of that under review, limiting the hours in which grown and intelligent men may labor to earn their living, are mere meddlesome interferences with the rights of the individual...

Source: Theodore Roosevelt, "The New Nationalism," 1910

I stand for the square deal. But when I say I am for the square deal, I mean not merely that I stand for fair play under the present rules of the game, but that I stand for having those rules changed so as to work for a more substantial equality of opportunity and of reward for equally good service ... But I think we may go still further. The right to regulate the use of wealth in the public interest is universally admitted. Let us admit also the right to regulate the terms and conditions of labor, which is the chief element of wealth, directly in the interest of the common good. The fundamental thing to do for every man is to give him a chance to reach a place in which he will make the greatest possible contribution to the public welfare.

This New Nationalism regards the executive power [of the federal government] as the steward of the public welfare. It demands of the judiciary that it shall be interested primarily in human welfare rather than in property, just as it demands that the representative body [Congress] shall represent all the people rather than any one class or section of the people.

Suggested Ideas about the Changing Role of Government

Changing Philosophy and Causes:

- abandoned rigid laissez-faire and adopted a more active intervention in the economy

- the growth of big business put pressure on the government to do more

- the size of the government grew as did its workforce

- agriculture as a percentage of the workforce declined 1880- 50% 1910- 31%

- manufacturing became more important workforce 1880-23% 1910- 29%

- service jobs grew from 1880 – 8% to 1910- 10%

- writers and politicians encouraged the government to adopt a more active role in the economy

- the Depression of 1893 heightened calls for more government action

- the government rejected radical programs for monetary reform (free silver)

Government Action:

- greater use of the Sherman Anti-Trust act after 1901

- more government regulation of the economy. (Pure Food and Drug Act, Meat Inspection Act, etc.)

- progressive presidents (Roosevelt, Taft and Wilson) took the lead in expanding role of the government in the economy

- government action was held back by a conservative Supreme Court

Appendices

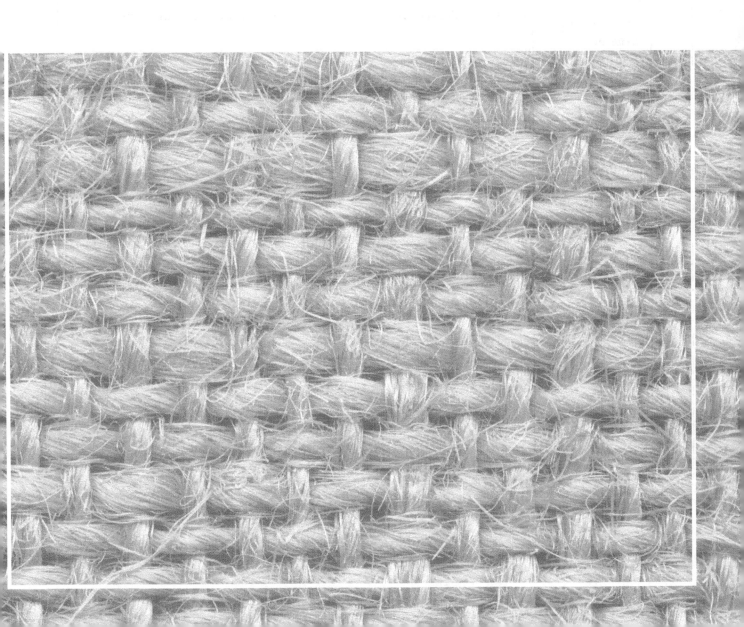

Rubric Guides

A Guide to Using the New Long Essay Rubric

Updated August 2015 to reflect most recent changes from the College Board

First, understand the LEQ six-point scale:

A	**Thesis** (1 point)	1 point for a strong **thesis** that makes a defensible claim and deals with all parts of the question.
B	Argument Development: **Targeted Historical Thinking Skill** (2 points)	1 point for **describing**, according to the HTS under consideration.
		1 point for **explaining** reasons/extent, according to the HTS, with more examples and analysis.
C	Argument Development: **Using Evidence** (2 points)	1 point for **addressing the topic** with examples of relevant evidence.
		1 point for utilizing a **broad range** of examples to **fully substantiate** (justify) the thesis or argument.
D	**Synthesis** (1 point)	1 point for connecting argument to ONE of the following: - a **development** in a different period, situation, era, geographic area. **(or)** - a course **theme** and/or approach to history that is not the focus of the essay (political, economic, social, cultural, intellectual).

Secondly, use the simplified grading checklist:

			0 points	1 point
A	**Thesis**	Makes defensible claim; deals with all parts of question		
B	Argument Development: **Targeted Historical Thinking Skill**	Describes according to the targeted skill		
		Explains reasons/extent, according to targeted skill		
C	Argument Development: **Using Evidence**	Addresses topic (some examples)		
		Justifies thesis, fully (broad range of examples)		
D	**Synthesis**	Connects argument to a different period/era/area or theme/approach		
			Total Score:	

After some practice, you should be able to use this quick scan table:
(circle the appropriate number)

Thesis	0 points	1 point	
Argument Development: **HTS**	0 points	1 point	2 points
Argument Development: **Evidence**	0 points	1 point	2 points
Synthesis	0 points	1 point	
		Total Score:	

A Guide to Using the New DBQ Rubric

Updated August 2015 to reflect most recent changes from the College Board

First, understand the DBQ seven-point scale:

A	**Thesis** (1 point)	1 point for presenting a **thesis** that makes a historically defensible claim and addresses all parts of the question.
	Argument Development (1 point)	1 point for recognizing/accounting for complexity by showing **relationships among evidence**, such as contradiction, corroboration and/or qualification.
B	**Document Analysis** (2 points)	1 point for utilizing **six** documents in argument.
		1 point for explaining the significance of ONE of the following for **four** documents: context, point of view, purpose, and/or audience.
C	**Using Evidence Beyond the Documents** (2 points)	1 point for connecting argument to broader events or processes immediately relevant to the question (**contextualization**).
		1 point for providing information outside of what is contained in the documents (old idea of **outside information**).
D	**Synthesis** (1 point)	1 point for connecting argument to ONE of the following: - a **development** in a different period, situation, era, geographic area, **(or)** - a course **theme** and/or approach to history that is not the focus of the essay (political, economic, social, cultural, intellectual).

Secondly, use the simplified grading checklist:

			0 points	1 point
A	**Thesis & Argument Dev.**	Makes defensible claim; addresses all parts of question		
		Shows contradiction, corroboration, qualification		
B	**Document Analysis**	Uses 6 documents		
		Explains ONE of the document aspects in 4 documents		
C	**Using Evidence Beyond Documents**	Connects argument to broader events		
		Provides outside information		
D	**Synthesis**	Connects argument to a different period/era/area or theme		
			Total Score:	

After some practice, you should be able to use this quick scan table:
(circle the appropriate number)

Thesis/Argument Development	0 points	1 point	2 points
Document Analysis	0 points	1 point	2 points
Contextualization/ Outside Evidence	0 points	1 point	2 points
Synthesis	0 points	1 point	
		Total Score:	

B

Distribution of Items by Chronological Period

Time Periods	Core Chart Questions	Source Activities Multiple-Choice	Source Activities Short-Answer	LEQs & DBQs
1491–1607	*Questions from this period can be found in the online testbank.*			
1607–1754	2.3; 3.1, 2, 3; 5.1, 2	3.1, 2	3.a, b, c	LEQ 1; DBQ 1
1754–1800	2.2; 10.1; 6.1, 2, 3; 13.1; 7.2; 16.2; 8.1, 2; 18.1	2.1, 2; 6.1, 2; 7.2	2.a, b; 6.a, b, c	LEQ 3
1800–1848	1.1; 13.2; 2.1; 14.1, 2, 3; 4.3; 15.1; 5.3; 16.3; 7.1, 3; 19.1, 2, 3; 11.3; 20.1, 2, 3; 12.2; 21.3	4.1, 2; 25.1; 5.1, 2; 27.1; 10.1, 2; 30.1; 12.1, 2; 35.1, 2; 14.1; 16.1, 2; 20.1, 2;	4.a, b, c; 20.a, b, c 5.a, b, c; 7.a, b, c; 10.a, b; 12.a; 13.a, b, c; 14.a, b;	LEQ 4, 7, 8, 10
1844–1877	10.2, 3; 18.2; 13.3; 21.1, 2; 16.1; 23.1, 2, 3	1.1, 2; 21.2; 13.1, 2; 23.1, 2; 18.1, 2; 32.2 21.1;	1.a, b, c; 21.a, b 16.a, b; 19.a, b, c;	LEQ 6; DBQ 2
1865–1898	1.3; 22.1; 4.1, 2; 24.1, 2, 3; 8.3; 25.1, 2, 3; 17.1; 26.1, 2, 3	7.1; 24.1, 2; 8.1, 2; 25.1, 2; 11.1, 2; 26.1, 2 21.1;	11.a, b, c; 14.c; 23.a, b, c; 25.a, b	LEQ 11
1890–1945	1.2; 22.3; 9.1; 27.1, 3; 12.1, 3; 28.1, 2, 3; 15.2, 3; 30.1, 2, 3; 17.3; 31.1, 2, 3	9.2; 31.1, 2 14.2; 15.2; 28.1, 2; 29.1;	8.a, b, c; 26.a, b; 12.b; 28.a; 15.a, b, c; 30.a, b, c; 16.c; 31.a, b, c; 21.c; 35.b	LEQ 9, 12, 13, 14, 15; DBQ 3
1945–1980	9.2; 29.1, 2, 3; 11.1, 2; 32.1, 2, 3; 17.2; 33.1, 2, 3; 18.3; 34.1, 2, 3; 22.2; 35.1, 2, 3 27.2;	17.1, 2; 33.1, 2; 19.1, 2; 34.1, 2 22.1, 2; 27.2; 30.2; 32.1;	9.b; 29.a, b, c; 17.a, b, c; 32.a, b, c; 22.a, b, c; 33.a, b, c; 24.a, b, c; 34.a, b, c 27.a, b, c; 28.b;	LEQ 5, 16, 17
1980–Present	9.3	9.1; 29.2	9.a;	LEQ 2

Distribution of Items by Learning Objective

Learning Objective	Source Activities				LEQs & DBQs
	Multiple-Choice		**Short-Answer**		
NAT-1	6.1, 2; 14.2; 16.1;	19.1; 21.1; 23.2	3.c; 5.a, b, c; 6.a, b, c; 12.a;	16.a; 21.b, c; 28.a	LEQ 1; DBQ 1
NAT-2	18.1; 23.1; 24.1, 2;	28.1; 32.1	24.a, b, c;	28.b	LEQ 11
NAT-3	34.1, 2;	35.2			
NAT-4			1.b;	27.c	
POL-1	2.1; 4.1, 2; 9.1, 2;	10.1, 2; 18.2; 19.2	1.c; 4.a, b, c; 9.a, b;	10.a; 14.a; 32.a, b, c	LEQ 2, 3, 4, 6
POL-2	2.2; 8.1, 2; 14.1;	20.1, 2; 21.2; 34.1, 2	2.a, b; 8.a, b; 10.b; 19.b;	20.a, b, c; 21.a; 34.a, b, c	LEQ 8, 10, 13, 14, 16; DBQ 2
POL-3	1.1, 2; 7.1, 2; 13.2; 14.2; 25.2;	26.2; 28.2; 29.1, 2; 31.1, 2; 32.1	1.a; 7.a, b, c; 8.c; 13.a, b, c; 14.b, c;	23.a, b; 26.a, b; 29.a, b, c; 31.a, b, c	LEQ 2, 5, 7, 11, 12 DBQ 3
WXT-1	11.1, 2;	13.1			
WXT-2	12.2; 25.1;	26.1; 30.1, 2	11.a, b, c; 19.c;	25.a, b; 30.a, b, c	LEQ 9, 15, 17
CUL-1	3.1, 2;	5.1, 2	7.a;	19.a, b	
CUL-4	27.1, 2		27.a, b		
WOR-1	12.1		12.b;	16.a	
WOR-2	15.1, 2; 16.2; 17.1, 2; 22.1, 2;	30.1, 2; 33.1, 2; 35.1	15.a, b, c; 16.c; 17.a, b, c; 22.a, b, c;	30.a, b, c; 33.a, b, c; 35.a, b, c	

Updated August 2016

Explanation of Numbering System:
    "19.1" refers to Lesson 19, multiple-choice question 1.
    "22.a, c" refers to Lesson 24, short-answer question parts a and c.

Distribution Charts

Distribution of Items by Historical Thinking Skill

Skill Type	Historical Thinking Skills	Source Activities		LEQs & DBQs
		Multiple-Choice	**Short-Answer**	
Chronological Reasoning	Historical Causation	2.2; 3.2; 5.2; 8.2; 9.1; 11.1; 12.1; 14.1; 15.1, 2; 16.2; 17.2; 18.2; 19.2; 20.2; 22.2; 23.1, 2; 24.1; 25.1; 26.1, 2; 27.2; 29.2; 30.2; 31.1; 32.1; 33.1, 2; 34.2; 35.1, 2	2.b; 3.c; 4.a; 5.a, b, c; 8.c; 10.a; 16.b; 19.c; 23.c; 27.c; 30.a, c; 32.a; 33.a; 35.b	LEQ 1, 5, 6, 7, 11, 14, 16; DBQ 1, 2, 3
	Patterns of Continuity and Change over Time	5.1; 7.1, 2; 9.2; 10.1; 11.2; 13.1; 14.2; 16.1; 18.1; 19.1; 21.2; 23.2; 25.2; 26.2; 28.2; 29.1, 2; 30.1; 31.1, 2; 34.1; 35.1	2.a; 7.c; 9.a; 14.c; 16.c; 21.c; 22.c; 35.c	LEQ 1, 4, 5, 6, 7, 8, 12, 14, 15; DBQ 1, 2, 3
	Periodization	1.2;	32.b, c; 33.b	LEQ 9
Comparison and Contextualization	Comparison	4.2; 32.2	12.b; 20.c; 29.b	LEQ 2, 3, 10, 13, 17
	Contextualization	6.2; 10.2; 14.1; 24.2; 30.1; 31.2; 32.2; 33.1	21.c; 22.c; 23.a; 30.c; 33.c	
Crafting Historical Arguments from Historical Evidence	Historical Argumentation		22.a	
	Appropriate Use of Relevant Historical Evidence	1.1; 2.1; 4.1; 3,1; 6.1; 8.1; 12.2; 13.2; 17.1; 20.1; 21.1; 22.1; 24.2; 25.1; 27.1; 28.1	1.a; 4.b, c; 6.a, c; 7.a, b; 9.b; 10.b; 11.a, c; 12.a; 13.a, c; 14.a, b; 15.c; 16.a; 17.a, b, c; 19.a, b, c; 20.a, c; 21.a; 24.a, c; 25.a; 26.a, c; 27.a, b; 28.a, b; 29.a, c; 30.b; 31.a, c; 32.c; 33.c; 34.a, c; 35.a	DBQ 1, 2, 3

Applying the Common Core State Standards©

The Common Core State Standards for 11th and 12th grade History and Social Studies revolve entirely around the use of primary and secondary sources, making *Threads* a useful tool for integrating the standards into your existing curriculum. The chart below identifies where each standard is directly addressed in one or more of the practice items; **boldface** indicates that the lesson as a whole addresses the standard in a larger way.

English Language Arts Standards — History and Social Studies, Grades 11–12			
Key Ideas and Details:	Lessons	**Integration of Knowledge and Ideas:**	Lessons
CCSS.ELA-LITERACY.RH.11-12.1 Cite specific textual evidence to support analysis of primary and secondary sources, connecting insights gained from specific details to an understanding of the text as a whole.	1, 4, 6, 7, 12, 13, 14, 17, 19, 21, 24-34	**CCSS.ELA-LITERACY.RH.11-12.7** Integrate and evaluate multiple sources of information presented in diverse formats and media (e.g., visually, quantitatively, as well as in words) in order to address a question or solve a problem.	**16;** DBQs 1-3
CCSS.ELA-LITERACY.RH.11-12.2 Determine the central ideas or information of a primary or secondary source; provide an accurate summary that makes clear the relationships among the key details and ideas.	4, 7, 14, 16, 20, 22, 23, 27, 30, 35	**CCSS.ELA-LITERACY.RH.11-12.8** Evaluate an author's premises, claims, and evidence by corroborating or challenging them with other information.	4, 24, 28, **34**
CCSS.ELA-LITERACY.RH.11-12.3 Evaluate various explanations for actions or events and determine which explanation best accords with textual evidence, acknowledging where the text leaves matters uncertain.	2, 3, 5, 8, 16, 19, 23, 27, 30, 32, 33, 35	**CCSS.ELA-LITERACY.RH.11-12.9** Integrate information from diverse sources, both primary and secondary, into a coherent understanding of an idea or event, noting discrepancies among sources.	**16,** 19, 28; DBQs 1-3
Craft and Structure:	Lessons	**Range of Reading and Level of Text Complexity:**	Lessons
CCSS.ELA-LITERACY.RH.11-12.4 Determine the meaning of words and phrases as they are used in a text, including analyzing how an author uses and refines the meaning of a key term over the course of a text (e.g., how Madison defines faction in Federalist No. 10).	**8, 9,** 18, 28	**CCSS.ELA-LITERACY.RH.11-12.10** By the end of grade 12, read and comprehend history/social studies texts in the grades 11-CCR text complexity band independently and proficiently.	1-35
CCSS.ELA-LITERACY.RH.11-12.5 Analyze in detail how a complex primary source is structured, including how key sentences, paragraphs, and larger portions of the text contribute to the whole.	3, 4, 14, 16, **18,** 27, 35		
CCSS.ELA-LITERACY.RH.11-12.6 Evaluate authors' differing points of view on the same historical event or issue by assessing the authors' claims, reasoning, and evidence.	5, 10, 11, 15-17, 21, 22, 27, 31, 33, 34		

SHERPALEARNING
GUIDING YOU TO EVEN GREATER HEIGHTS

Our mission is to open doors for high-achieving learners through access to high-quality, skills-based instruction written by rock-star teachers.

Threads of History
2nd Edition

Don't miss out on the

Teacher's Companion Website

Purchase of this Teacher's Companion Resource includes free access to the Teacher's Companion Website. In order to access the materials, you will need to register for an account using the unique ID code found on the inside front cover of this text. The following are just some of the valuable resources you'll find on the site:

- Printable and downloadable formats for the 17 Long Essay Questions and 3 Document-Based Questions, as well as answer sheet templates that simulate the exam

- H.I.P.P.O. DBQ Planning Worksheet - ready to print

- 150+ Multiple-Choice review questions with detailed answer analysis in a convenient sort and filter display; use these questions to test student comprehension in the various historical periods so you can identify areas requiring more intensive review

- Core Chart Worksheets for building students' synthesis and summarization skills

- Perhaps most importantly, critical updates to the content found in the Student Edition and this Companion Resource! (As the College Board makes changes to the AP U.S. History curriculum, we update our content.)

Go to http://threads.sherpalearning.com to register today!

Note to Teachers and Administrators

We at Sherpa Learning hope to continue to create amazing content at sensible prices for years to come. But we're a small crew of believers with no corporate umbrella to hide under. As such, we'd ask that you consider buying a class set if you can afford it. We understand that times are tough and that sometimes you just have to do what you have to do. The students come first. But it's hard for a company like ours to survive selling one book at a time. Just keep it in mind. That's all we ask.

And if you loved this book, check out our site for other amazing resources. Don't forget to register with the site to become a contributor, stay informed about new AP resources, and be part of the leadership conversation.

www.sherpalearning.com